LOCKHEED P-38 LIGHTNING

A flight of P-38 Lightnings, 1st FG, 27th FS, US 15th Air Force.

Classic WWII Aviation

LOCKHEED
P-38 LIGHTNING

Terry C. Treadwell

CERBERUS

Published in 2003

PUBLISHED IN THE UNITED KINGDOM BY:

Cerberus Publishing Limited
Penn House, Leigh Woods
Bristol BS8 3PF
Telephone: ++44 117 974 7175
Facsimile: ++44 117 973 0890
e-mail: cerberusbooks@aol.com

British Library Cataloguing in Publication Data.
A catalogue record for this book is available from the British Library.

ISBN 1 84145 109 6

PRINTED AND BOUND IN UK

Contents

Series Introduction

Many different types of aircraft were involved in the Second World War, new, old, conventional, and some, downright bizarre. Any selection in a series of 'classic' aircraft will, therefore, always be arbitrary and subject to the views of individuals. The selection of aircraft for this series has been primarily governed by their operational importance, although some types have, by necessity, other claims for inclusion. The series also seeks to cover a wide spectrum of the different operations involved during the conflict as well as those countries that had a leading role.

The major powers, during the 1930s, were becoming increasingly aware that the political instability throughout the world would inevitably lead to military conflict. The advent of Adolf Hitler's rise to power in Germany, and the increasing strength of the new Luftwaffe, led many nations to the realization that to rely on their air forces' existing capabilities would be extremely unwise and that they had to expand and re-equip with more modern combat aircraft. However, despite this obvious threat no country, at the outbrak of the Second World War, had the numerical strength or modern equipment to compare with that of the Luftwaffe.

The Spanish Civil War (1936-1939) afforded several of the major air powers, particularly Germany and Italy, an ideal opportunity to put their newly designed aircraft to the test under battle conditions. The pilots of Germany's *Legion Condor* and Italy's *Aviazione Legionaria* evolved a number of strategies that were utilized in the early part of the Second World War and the senior officers of the Luftwaffe were quick to realize the need for specialized ground-attack aircraft. On the other hand, the often inferior opposition and the ease with which they were eliminated, gave the German and Italian aircrews, as well as the officials of their respective air forces, an over-estimated view of the superiority of their aircraft.

The Messerschmitt Bf109 had been conceived in the flush of Hitler's take-over of power in 1933, and as a monoplane had complete superiority in the air until the appearance of the Spitfire. Yet the Bf 109E, the 'Emil', which provided the main fighter force for Germany during the first year of the Second World War, including the Battle of Britain period, had not evolved significantly from the Bf 109C which was the predominant fighter aircraft used by the Luftwaffe in the Spanish Civil War. Italy's pilots had a totally different concept and still preferred the open cockpit and light armoury that would allow them to out-manoeuvre their opponants.

During the immediate pre-war years the peacetime expansion of the Royal Air Force, by comparison with Germany, was slow and hampered by financial restraints. Like Italy, Britain was reluctant to dispense with their bi-plane fighters until the monoplane had proved itself. Although the manufacturers of Britain's two monoplane developments, the Hurricane and the Spitfire, were given substantial pre-war orders the RAF, at the outbreak of war, had little more than 300 Hurricanes in first-line service and approximately 150 Spitfires – less than a tenth of those ordered. In 1938, and with the war clouds gathering, the RAF's weakness was only too apparent and a delegation, the British Purchasing Mission, went to the United States to order substantial quantities of US combat aircraft in an attempt to fill the gap. Most of these aircraft were not delivered until sometime in 1940 and the RAF had to supplement their inferior numbers of Hurricanes and Spitfires with the bi-plane Gloster Gladiator and the near obsolescent Fairey Battle, which were no match for the 'Emil'.

The Soviet Union, although on paper, were numerically strong, its front-line aircraft were anything but modern as it was still in the early stages of a modernization program. Like Britain and France the Soviet Union was relying on aircraft from the United States.

The Japanese, like the Italians, seemed to have a prediliction for open cockpits and lightly armed, but highly manoeuvrable, aircraft. However, they discarded the bi-plane somewhat earlier and, at the time they opened hostilities against the United States, all principle first-line Army and Navy fighters were monoplanes, including the Mitsubishi Zero-Sen.

At the time of Pearl Harbor, in December 1941, the United States' aviation industry was already heavily involved in the production of aircraft for Britain and other countries. This was now substantially increased by the demands of their own forces. Nevertheless output, from 1941 to 1945, included over 12,000 Mustangs, 12,000 Corsairs, 15,000 Thunderbolts and 20,000 Hellcats and Wildcats. In addition over 12,500 B-17s were produced together with over 18,000 B-24 Liberators.

The Classic WWII Aviation series is designed to give a comprehensive history of many of the aircraft used during this period and each title will cover the prototype development, production and operational use of the aircraft in service with the main protagonists. The series will cover fighter aircraft, heavy, medium and light bombers, in narrative text, many black and white photographs with line and colour drawings to show the different types of aircraft, squadron and unit colour schemes.

Introduction

This book is about one of the most respected and feared fighters of the Second World War - the Lockheed P-38 Lightning. Throughout the war, but mainly in the Pacific and Mediterranean Theatres, the P-38s of the USAAC caused havoc with the enemy and became known to the Germans as the *Der Gabelschwanz Teufel* or `Fork-Tailed Devil'.

It was P-38 Lightnings from the 18th and 347th Fighter Groups, that attacked and destroyed the 'Betty' bomber carrying Admiral Isoroku Yamamoto, causing great concern within the Japanese military hierarchy as Yamamoto was deemed to be the Japanese Navy's top naval strategist. It was Yamamoto who was the architect of the attack on Pearl Harbor on 7 December 1941

The P-38 Lightning was never intended to be a fighter combatant, but an interceptor and destroyer of bombers. In reality it was a flying anti-aircraft weapon. It is said to have destroyed more Japanese aircraft than any other US aircraft.

When the Boeing B-17s and other heavy bombers struggled home after a raid in the first part of the war, it was the welcoming sight of the P-38 Lightnings arriving to fly cover for the straggling, damaged bombers, that often met them.

This is not the definitive work on this remarkable aircraft, but hopefully it will give the reader a new insight into its relatively short but highly productive life.

CHAPTER ONE

...of unusual design.

In January 1937 the United States Army Air Corps (USAAC) put on their 'wanted' list an aircraft for the tactical mission of interception and attack of hostile aircraft at high altitudes. The aircraft had to have a true airspeed of 360 mph at high altitude and have a climb rate that could take it to 20,000 feet in six minutes. It also had to have a take-off and landing distance of 2,200 feet and be able to clear a 50 feet obstacle at the end of a runway. This immediately moved the requirement from a single-engine to a twin-engine aircraft as there was not a single engine in production at the time that had

Lockheed's first management group L-R: Lloyd Stearman (President); Robert Gross (Chairman); Cyril Chappellet (Secretary) and Hall L. Hibbard (Vice-President and Chief Engineer).

sufficient power to meet these stringent requirements. This in itself created another obstacle, as with the additional fuel required to power the two engines, the weight of the aircraft became a major factor in the design.

A number of aircraft companies including Consolidated, Vultee, Douglas, Curtiss and Lockheed were invited to submit designs for consideration. One of the aircraft manufacturers, Lockheed, had only been in existence as an aircraft manufacturer since 1927 having been founded by Allan Lockheed, Malcolm Lockheed, Fred Keeler, John Northrop and W K Jay. However, this distinguished collection of men had control of the company for only two years before selling out to a group from Detroit, who, within a very short time, went into receivership brought on in the main by the Great Depression of 1929. An upturn in the stock market in 1932 brought new investors into the aviation world and Lockheed's assets were purchased for $40,000. The new owners were an investment banker Robert E Gross, Lloyd Stearman, Thomas Ryan III -- who owned Mid-Continent Airlines, an investment broker E C Walker and Mr and Mrs Cyril Chappellet.

One of the first engineers brought into the company was Hall L Hibbard who had previously worked for Lloyd Stearman and who was later to be responsible for the development of the very successful Lockheed Model 10 Electra. Hibbard in turn brought in Clarence L `Kelly' Johnson. They had first met when Hibbard had sent a scale model of the Model 10 Electra to the wind tunnel facility at the University of Michigan for tests. Kelly Johnson carried out the tests and wrote a very critical report on the aircraft tail assembly. The depth of the report impressed Hibbard so much that he offered Kelly Johnson a job with the new company, a decision which was to prove to be a very important one for Lockheed at that time and for many years to come.

Model 10 Electra

The USAAC's specifications for the new aircraft were passed to Lockheed's team of young designers headed by Hall L Hibbard, now promoted to be Lockheed's Chief Engineer, and his assistant Kelly Johnson. Johnson in later years would head Lockheed's famous secret `Skunk Works'.

This was a giant step for the Lockheed company, as they had never built a military aircraft that was to go into series production before and never one with the specifications that were laid down. Many people thought that the company was over-stretching itself, but the President of the company at the time, Robert E Gross, had other ideas.

Kelly Johnson produced freehand sketches of a number of designs and within days the design team had narrowed the selection down to six and produced a series of preliminary drawings and specifications. These included one design that concealed both engines in the fuselage, and by a series of shafts and gears through the wings, operated the propellers. This was deemed to be far too complex and was discarded. Another used the pusher engines in the fuselage and a tail consisting of twin fins and rudders. One of Kelly Johnson's sketches bore a close resemblance to an interceptor that would appear some years later, the McDonald XP-67 `Bat'.

Using a push-pull engine mounted forward and aft of the cockpit was another idea, but the idea accepted by all was the proposal for the Lockheed X608 design, Model 22. This was a twin-engine, twin-fuselage, twin-tail,

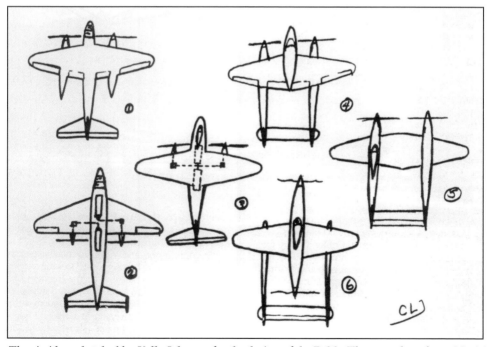

The six ideas sketched by Kelly Johnson for the design of the P-38. The one selected was No.4.*

single-seat fighter with a tricycle undercarriage. The pilot, armament and nose landing gear was housed in a tiny fuselage mounted between the twin boom fuselage on the wing center-line. The proposal was delivered personally by Lockheed's President Robert Gross to the Army at Wright Field, Dayton, Ohio. Four months later on June 23, 1937, the proposal was approved by the Army. The company was given the Air Corps Contract No. 9974 for one aircraft, together with a stipulation that the engines to be used in the aircraft were made by the Allison Company. Designated the XP-38 and given the Air Corps number of 37-457, the actual construction of the aircraft did not start until July 1938.

The reasoning behind the choice of engine manufacturers was that some years earlier the Army had become convinced that there was a need for a turbo-charged, high-powered, liquid-cooled engine and had invested money into a development fund with the Allison company.

The Allison company had started life as a specialist engineering company in Indianapolis, Indiana and whose chief engineer Norman H Gilman, had developed a new fine-grained bronze coated steel bearing in 1915, which extended the life of engines by a factor of ten. Within months the company was supplying most of America's engine manufacturers with bearings which made the company very financially viable. With funds to support them, the Company started to look at developing their own engines beginning with the creation of a radically new marine yacht engine. Three years later, the founder James Allison died and the Allison Engineering Company was purchased by Captain Eddie Rickenbacker, America's leading fighter ace in the First World War. Then in 1928 he sold it to the Fisher Brothers who, together with Norman Gilman, developed a new V-12 aero engine. Recognising the development and potential of the new engine the General Motors Company made a successful bid for the Allison Engineering Company a few months later and Allisons became one of its subsidiaries. The company had been carrying out the development on the V-12 since 1932, which culminated in the arrival of the V-1710-C8 just as the Model 22 project was accepted by the USAAC.

Such was the exact design specifications of the aircraft, that it was interesting to note that the wingspan, 52 feet (15.84 m), the wing area, 327.5 sq. ft (30.42 m²), length, 37ft 10ins. (11.53 m) and height, 12ft 10in. (3.91 m), remained almost the same throughout all the variations and models. The V-1710-C8 engine appeared to be tailor-made for the P-38 and fitted in exactly with the required specifications.

In the early hours of New Years Day 1939, three trucks, with their loads completely covered with canvas, left the Lockheed plant at Burbank,

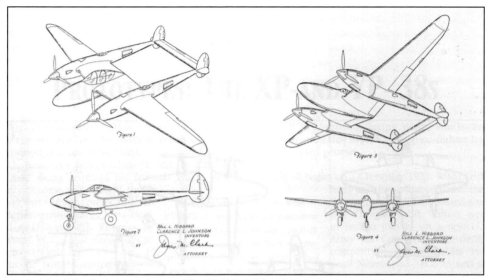

A sketch of the design put forward by Hall L Hibbard and Clarence L Johnson.

California under a heavy military and plant security escort and went to March Field, near Riverside, California. There, under the strictest secrecy, the three trucks were unloaded and their cargoes placed in a hangar. Nine days later a re-assembled XP-38 was ready for its first test flight and was to be flown by Lieutenant Benjamin S Kelsey, USAAC. Kelsey was an extremely experienced pilot and had been assigned as the XP-38 project officer by the Army.

On the day of the first tests Lieutenant Benjamin Kelsey slid himself into the cockpit of the aircraft, completely familiar with all the controls as he had spent hours in the cockpit during the aircraft's construction. The two big Allison V-1710-C9 engines grumbled, then roared into life one by one and Kelsey watched first as the left-hand Curtiss Electric propeller rotated clockwise, then the right-hand propeller rotated anti-clockwise (both rotating inwards). The reason for this was to help counter the effects of the torque and the propeller wash that emanated from them. (In all subsequent models of the P-38 the propellers rotated outwards).

Releasing the brakes, Kelsey started on a series of taxi tests and it soon became obvious that the brakes were inadequate. This was highlighted when, during one high speed taxi run, the aircraft ran out of runway when the wheels expanded with heat and braking power was lost. The aircraft ended up in a ditch, but fortunately suffered little damage. An auxiliary hand brake system was developed by using a cylinder from a Northrop A-17, together with an additional hydraulic oil tank. The idea was that when the brakes started to fade the pilot would pump additional hydraulic

Lieutenant Ben Kelsey with a model of the YP-38.

oil into the braking system. It was soon realised that even using this system, after two landings the brakes would be gone and was also a totally unsatisfactory method of braking. Lt Kelsey decided to land the aircraft without using the wheel brakes.

To do this he would have to make a long low approach, and using just enough power to keep the aircraft from stalling, cut the power the moment the runway appeared under the nose of the aircraft. It worked – but it wasn't satisfactory. The system could be used during tests, but this was a military aircraft that would have to operate under battle conditions. The problem needed to be solved and quick.

The first test flight of the aircraft also uncovered some other problems. Just after take-off a severe flutter developed in the wings. So severe in fact that there was an up and down movement at the wingtip of around two to three feet. Kelsey retracted the newly fitted Fowler flaps and almost immediately the flutter stopped. It was discovered later that three of the aluminium flap-control link rods had broken, which allowed the flaps to go to the end of their travel and flap around loose. The problem was resolved

YP-38 with Lockheed Chief Test Pilot Marshall Headle taxiing out for a test flight.

by replacing the aluminium rods with ones made of steel. It was later discovered that the flap arrangement, when placed on the half-flap setting on take-off and the full-flap setting on landing, was subjected to buffeting. This meant that the engines had to be cut just prior to lowering the flaps for landing. Kelly Johnson discovered that the airflow at the leading edge of the flaps was being `pinched off', so he cut holes in the skin of the well that housed the flaps and solved the problem. This modification was only carried out on the YP-38 much later.

Although there was a real need for the aircraft to be operational only five hours of flying were accomplished in the next two weeks. There were no major problems as such just minor niggling ones that seemed to take forever to solve. One of these was to instrumental in the demise of the XP-38, when later it was suspected that the early turbosuperchargers were not producing enough carburettor heat to combat carburettor ice when running at a low rpm.

Then disaster struck. In Washington, General Henry H 'Hap' Arnold, Chief of the Air Corps, who was negotiating with the Congressional Appropriation Committee for more funds, found himself being put under pressure by some members of the committee regarding the record breaking British Supermarine Spitfire and the German Messerschmitt Me 109. They felt that America should be able to compete on the same level. It was decided to use the speed of the XP-38 to demonstrate to the other members of the appropriation committee, the justification for the demand for more funding.

Lieutenant Kelsey was ordered to deliver the XP-38 to Wright Field via Amarillo, Texas. It was decided at Wright Field to try and break Howard

The XP-38 the first of the Lightnings

Hughes coast-to-coast record of 7 hours 26 minutes by flying from March Field, California, to Mitchel Field, Long Island, New York. It was thought, if successful, it would give General Arnold some leverage when he next went in front of the appropriation committee to ask for additional funding. The flight went well and averaged 360 mph for the flight. After 7 hours and 43 minutes and two refuelling stops at Amarillo, Texas and Wright Field, Dayton, Ohio, Kelsey made his approach to Mitchel Field. As he was on the long, slow, low-level final approach his engine power failed. Unable to maintain height he sliced through the top of a tree and ended up in a ditch on a golf course close to the airfield. The aircraft was completely destroyed, fortunately the pilot was unhurt.

Some made relatively light of the accident, saying that it was the kind of thing that happens when testing new aircraft. What has to be remembered, was that this was the one and only model of this aircraft, unlike today when at least two prototypes are built. Lockheed were back to square one and had to start building a new aircraft from scratch. The accident was attributed to ice in the carburettors, which resulted in a complete re-design of the fuel system for the engine. A number of other modifications were made to the new design – the YP-38.

There were a number of scathing comments from experienced test pilots regarding the crash and the events that led up to it. The fact that a prototype

YP-38 with Lockheed Chief Test Pilot Marshall Headle taxiing out for a test flight.

was used to go after a transcontinental speed record was disturbing as far as they were concerned, because the only thing that anyone would get out of it were a few headlines. In their opinion the aircraft had not been properly tested and was still in its embryo stage compared to most other prototypes.

Lieutenant Kelsey reported to General Arnold in Washington and explained what happened and told him about the new design for the YP-38 which incorporated all the best features of the XP-38 and the improvements. General Arnold took Kelsey with him to meet the various civilian members of the Congressional Appropriation Committee and asked him to explain why the aircraft crashed and to `sell' them on the new model.

The only thing that did come out of the crash, was the fact that there was no prototype to criticise and the basic design and performance had proved that it was a worthwhile project. After listening to Kelsey extoll the virtues of the XP-38 the appropriation committee approved the additional funds for the YP-38.

Within two months, on 27 April 1939, Lockheed was given a $2 million order for thirteen service-test YP-38s under Air Force Contract 12523. The first YP-38 flew on 16 September 1940 and was flown by Lockheed's Chief Test Pilot, Marshall Headle. On de-briefing Headle declared, ' This is a very fast airplane and in all my experience as a pilot, it's the easiest plane I have

General `Hap' Arnold, USAAF, and Air Chief Marshal Sir Arthur Harris, RAF, conferring.

had to fly.'

The first of the production models was delivered to the USAAC on 11 March 1941 nine months before the fateful attack on Pearl Harbor by the Japanese. It was to be a further eight months before the last of the thirteen aircraft ordered were delivered. Five months into the contract, the USAAC negotiated with Lockheed for a further sixty-seven operational ready P-38s, six months later the order was increased and an additional 607 aircraft were requested. Even the British placed a tentative order for 667 P-38s (P-322s).

The YP-38 flown by Lockheed test pilot Marshall Headle, taking off on its initial test flight from the Lockheed facility at Burbank, California.

At the end of 1938 the Vega Airplane Company, a subsidiary of Lockheed, had purchased 30 acres of land next to the Union Air Terminal in California and built a manufacturing plant. The military version of the Electra Model 14, the Ventura bomber, which was destined for Britain, was built there. Versions of this aircraft were built for the USAAC (B-34 & B-37) and the US Navy (PV-1). This was one of the orders that was keeping the parent company viable and one that was to attract criticism from the US military.

The YP-38 on a test flight flown by Lockheed test pilot Marshall Headle.

Whilst waiting for the decision from the USAAC on whether or not they were going to purchase the P-38, the company had managed to keep their head above water with the production of an enlarged 14-seat midwing version of the Electra (Model 14) for, ironically, the Japan Air Line Company

The second of the prototype YP-38s in the wind tunnel at the NACA facility at the Langley Research Centre.

(*Dai Nippon*). It was fortunate because at the same time the British Purchasing Commission were desperately searching for a medium reconnaissance bomber and were due to visit the factory at the beginning of 1938. The British commission would most certainly not have given a contract to a company that was not in the throes of producing aircraft. A week before the arrival of the commission the company managed to produce a wooden mock-up of the Model 14 that had been converted to a medium reconnaissance bomber and renamed the Model 10A – it was just what the British were looking for. They were immediately impressed and placed an order for 250 of the aircraft at a total cost of $25 million, the largest single order ever placed with an American aircraft company. Over 3000 Model 10As, or Hudsons as they were called by the British, were eventually built and served with distinction throughout the war. The aircraft also served with the RAAF and the USAAC and given the designations A-28, A-29 and AT-18.

Suddenly the order from the USAAC for the P-38 came through. The problem now was that Lockheed company, still angry about the loss of the XP-38 because of the publicity stunt carried out by the USAAC, were not prepared for mass production of aircraft. Furthermore, because of the

The second prototype YP-38 at Wright Field, Dayton, Ohio.

military hardware that was needed to be installed inside the aircraft, a re-design was needed. The weight of the non-combatant YP-38 was 13,500 pounds, but the combat ready P-38, with the additional weight of the guns and ammunition, weighed in at 14,348 pounds. It is very easy to criticise the aircraft manufacturers at this time, but in reality no aircraft manufacturer was ready for the kind of mass production that was to become the `norm' within a very short period. There was not the manpower, money or the metal available to carry out mass production. In addition to this, there were priorities being given to other types of aircraft being built such as the Boeing B-17 bombers, Lockheed Hudsons and Venturas.

The YP-38, like the XP-38, had been hand-built and the design of the airframe did not lend itself to mass production. There were a number of modifications to be made before the aircraft could be put into operational production. By August 1941 39 P-38s, as they were now known, had been delivered and by November the figure had risen to 69. The USAAF (the United States Army Air Corps became the United States Army Air Force on 20 June 1941) blamed Lockheed for the slow delivery, stating that the company was still concentrating on the financial profits from the

Pre-production YP-38s in pre-war national markings and in a natural metal finish.

commercial Lodestar model and the orders from the British for the Lockheed Hudson. This was vehemently denied in no uncertain terms by the company.

Tests with the P-38 were still under way when the supercharger was introduced causing another set of problems. Severe tail flutter was being experienced by some pilots when the aircraft was at high speed. Even while this was being evaluated a new model, the P-38D, was going into production. There was another problem that affected the tail section and this was compressibility or `shock stall' as it was more commonly known. The problems were not related and so different solutions had to be found for them. As early as 1937 Kelly Johnson and Hall L Hibbard had warned of this problem and in a memorandum to Robert Gross, Hal Hibbard said:

> In order to to have the minimum possible drag, it is essential that air flows smoothly over any part of an aircraft's structure. As the speed is increased, the air tends to be `splashed' by the leading edge of the wing more or less like the prow of a boat at high speed in the water. As one approaches the compressability range, the air is thrown so violently up and down by the leading edge that it does not have a chance to flow over the wing in the proper manner.

A number of experiments were carried out, including placing weights in the tail section, but after weeks of testing it was discovered that there was nothing wrong with the tail design, it was attributed to a strong turbulent airflow. Changes to the aerodynamics of the aircraft included the redistribution of the elevator mass balances and the installation of new fillets where the fuselage and leading edges joined. Together with a dive brake that was attached to the main spar and which restored lift immediately to the underside of the wing the moment compressability started, solved the problem. The angle of incidence for the whole tailplane was also changed from 1º 15′ to 0º 0′ and was contributory in solving the tail flutter. The rotation of the propellers was changed from rotating inwards to both propellers rotating outwards making the aircraft considerably more stable.

The P-38 was not the only aircraft to suffer from severe tail flutter when in a high speed dive, a number of incidents were reported with the North

This high-tailed P-38 was developed in an effort to stop the compressibility problem but was unsuccessful.

American Mustang when it first appeared. Several Mustangs lost their tails when pushed beyond 400 miles per hour n level flight, as did the P-47 Thunderbolt which became known among some pilots as the `Widowmaker' because of the problem.

The P-38 Lightning was armed with one 23-mm Madsen cannon and four 0.5-inch electrically heated Colt machine guns, all mounted in the nose. The guns, together with their ammunition, pushed the weight of the aircraft to 15,340 lbs. Twenty-nine models of the P-38 were built and were produced between June 1941 and August 1941.

In August 1941 the XP-38A appeared. This was a modified P-38 that was fitted with a pressurised cockpit intended for use at high altitudes. It was sent to Wright Field in Ohio for evaluation, but was rejected on the grounds that the cost of converting and building aircraft with pressurised cockpits was not warranted. A decision that in later years was cursed by a number of P-38 pilots, some of whom had to turn back from combat missions because of the freezing cold they were experiencing at high altitudes. It was also armed with one 37-mm Oldsmobile cannon, two 0.5-inch Colt MG-53 machine guns and two Colt Mg-40 machine guns.

The first of the Lightning Mk Is (AF105) destined for the Royal Air Force arrived in Britain for evaluation at the beginning of 1942. In March 1940, the

RAF Lightning Mk.1 Model P-322, AE992 in US markings after being delivered to the RAF for evaluation.

British Purchasing Commission ordered an initial 143 P-38s (P-322s), all to be fitted with the 37-mm Hispano cannon in preference to the existing 20-mm preferred by the USAAC. The Lightning clearly looked a formidable piece of machinery, sleek, powerful, fast and deadly with four machine guns

One of the three British Lightnings No.AE979 on a test and evaluation flight in Britain.

and a cannon protruding from its nose. But as a philosopher once said: `Between precept and practice a great shadow falls'

The first of these P-38s was subjected to a series of stringent evaluation tests but did not impress the test pilots. The aircraft was handed back to the Americans by means of transferring it to the Eighth Air Force. Clearly the RAF test pilots had not read the script, because according to an extract from a 1934 Lockheed advertisement:

> *The pilots sent the P-38 climbing over eight miles straight towards the stratosphere, up to where even the highest flying bombers couldn't go. They brought it screaming down out of the clouds like forked vengeance. They jammed down the throttle and flew it faster than any fighter before...*

Even allowing for copywriter's tendency to oversell every product they come in contact with, this clearly was a blatant overstatement of the aircraft abilities.

The second of the P-38s (AF106), arrived a week later at the A&AEE

One of the three P-38 Lightnings No.AF106 given to the RAF on a test and evaluation flight.

(Aeroplane & Armament Experimental Establishment) at Boscombe Down, Wiltshire, this model however was fitted with power-boosted controls. The engines were not fitted with turbo-superchargers as the US government at the time considered them too secret for it to be risked over Germany, so their export to Britain was forbidden. (In fact the Germans had already developed their own turbo-superchargers by this time). Again the aircraft was subjected to stringent tests and underwent a series of minor modifications before that too was rejected and returned. The test pilots all agreed that it was a very pleasant aircraft to fly within the set parameters and handled well. Amongst their comments, were the following:

> *It had a clean configuration with gear and flaps up, the aircraft stalled at 98 mph and with gear and flaps down landed nicely at 78 mph.*
> *Entry into the cockpit required a ladder, due to the height of the wing from the ground. This could be dangerous if the engines were running at the time.*
> *The view from the cockpit, despite the heavy frames was good, although no bullet proof windscreen was fitted.*
> *The propeller pitch control was too far forward for satisfactory operation.*
> *The aircraft was quite pleasant to fly and flew itself off the ground.*
> *Top speed of the aircraft was not tested as it was restricted to 300 mph max.*

But this was not an aircraft to fly just for pleasure, this was a military killing machine and was not at all manoeuvrable when tested under simulated combat conditions.

A third P-38 (AF108) was delivered to the RAF and fared no better, before that too was transferred to the US 8th Air Force.

It would appear on the face of it that the RAF had rejected the aircraft without giving it full consideration, but it has to be remembered that the three P-38 Lightnings given to the RAF for evaluation were not the same model as those that decimated the Japanese in the Pacific. The RAF test pilots had rejected all three P-38 aircraft saying they were clearly unfit for combat duties. The aircraft were not fitted with superchargers, the engines being the conventionally blown early model 1,150-hp Allisons and the propellers rotated in the same direction unlike the American models whose propellers rotated in opposite directions.

Before the remainder of the 143 Lightning Mk Is could be delivered, the order was cancelled and the evaluated aircraft returned to the United States where they were placed into a training wing. It is interesting to note that the P-38 was originally called the `Lockheed Atlanta' by the Americans, but was given the name `Lightning' by the British. The name stuck even after the Royal Air Force rejected the aircraft as not suitable, stating that it was no improvement on their Westland Whirlwind which was already in operational service.

The majority of the aircraft that had been destined for the Royal Air Force were absorbed by the USAAF and retained the given designation of P-322. These aircraft were assigned to training squadrons and were also used for a variety of tests. To turn them into trainers the space behind the pilot was emptied of armour plating and radio equipment and a little `piggy' seat installed. There were no dual controls and the student, cramped into the

The production line manufacturing the P-322 without superchargers for the Royal Air Force. The three aircraft that were sent to Britain for evaluation were returned as not suitable bringing this production line to a halt and those aircraft that were completed were taken by the USAAF for training purposes.

little receptacle behind the pilot, watched with eager eyes as the instructor went through the control movements, frantically hoping he would be able to remember it all. Later some twenty P-38F models were converted into two-seat trainers. Because of the cramped position of the student, the instructors had to remember not to deliberately carry out any violent manoeuvres in an effort to torment their students, because in the event of the student vomiting, it would invariably be all over the instructor.

In October 1941 Lockheed produced the P-38E model. Two hundred and ten models were produced and almost immediately a large number were assigned to either training or test squadrons. Improvements between the production of each model was continuous and between the D and the E models there were almost 2,000 changes in redesign and modifications, many of them being minor. There were some major modifications, such as changing the 37-mm Oldsmobile cannon for a smaller 20-mm Hispano cannon. The smaller cannon had a much faster rate of fire and was capable of carrying more ammunition. The hollow-bladed Hamilton Standard Hydromatic propellers were replaced with the Curtiss Electric dural blades. The E-model was also the first to be manufactured on a planned assembly

Because of the cancellation of the production order the remaining `castrated' P-38 Lightnings were assigned to the USAAF for training and experimental duties.

line that enabled modifications to be made whilst still under construction. Previously any modifications were made in another part of the factory after the aircraft had been built.

Lockheed test pilot Jimmy Mattern dressed for a high-altitude test flight about to climb into the cockpit of a P-38 Lightning on a manufacturers test flight.

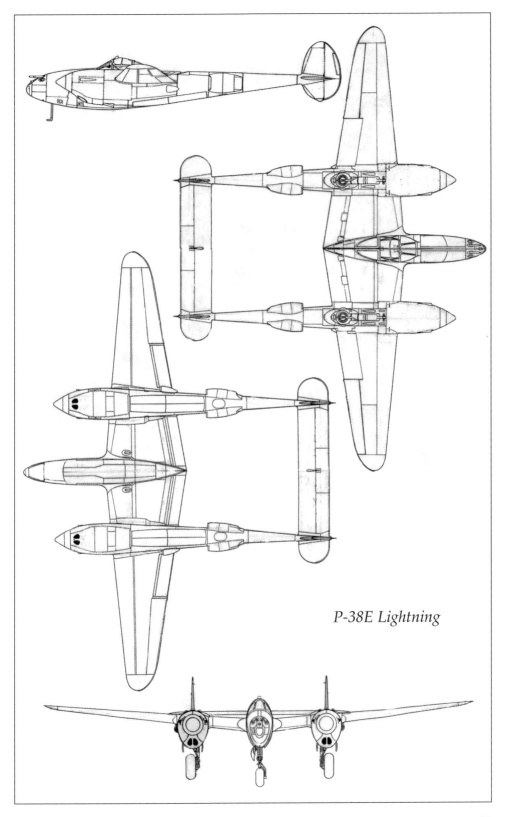

P-38E Lightning

Ninety-nine of the E-models were converted into F4-I-LO, unarmed, high-speed photo-reconnaissance aircraft. Four K-17 cameras were installed on each side of the aircraft and in the tip of the nose. In addition the aircraft was fitted with an automatic pilot, which was a real blessing for the pilots who flew the high-altitude, long-range missions.

Excellent head-on shot of a P-38E, with two drop-tanks, bearing down on the photo-shoot

Senior officers in the USAAF had looked very carefully at the need for these aircraft and had decided, wisely as it turned out, that there was a need for long range photo-reconnaissance aircraft. During the war in the Pacific, fast, high-altitude photo-reconnaissance flights deep into enemy held territory, using purpose built aircraft, cut down on the use of medium and heavy bombers being used for the same purpose. At the beginning of operations in the Pacific a small group of four aircraft belonging to 'A' Flight, 8th Photographic Squadron, under the command of Captain Kari Polifka, were stationed in Australia. Their aircraft were equipped with two 75-gallon auxiliary fuel tanks and cameras and, throughout the campaign, successfully carried out numerous missions, in all weathers, against horrendous odds. In fact of the 2,000 photo-reconnaissance aircraft in service with the AAF throughout the world, over 800 of them were either F-4 or F-5 variations of the P-38.

Although the Lightning was regarded as the ultimate multi-role aircraft

P-38E of No.1 Photographic Reconnaissance Unit, Royal Australian Air Force.

at the time, it did have certain drawbacks. When compared with the Japanese Zero, the Focke-Wulf Fw 190 and Messerschmitt Bf 109, it failed to measure up in regard to speed and manoeuvrability at low altitudes. At high altitudes, however, the P-38 came into its own with a higher rate of climb and a more powerful armament. Up to this point in time none of the Lockheed P-38 Lightnings were in regular squadrons, that was until the arrival of the P-38F.

The P-38 Lightning's development had a long list of accomplishments to its name. It was the first fighter aircraft of its time to be fitted with a tricycle undercarriage, the first to use turbo-superchargers that enabled it to fly at speeds in excess of 400 mph. Its twin-boom fuselage design was the first of its kind for a fighter of its day; the first American aircraft whose external surfaces were butt-jointed and flush riveted; the first to make extensive use of stainless steel in the construction of the aircraft and the first to mount all its guns ahead of the pilot enabling him to bring all his guns to bear at once on any target within range.

The turbo-supercharger was not a new invention. During the First World War a French engineer by the name of Professor A C E Rateau developed a gas-turbine driven supercharger When fitted to an aircraft engine it boosted the aircraft's performance considerably, achieving record altitudes. At the

P-38D Lightning parked in a sandbag protected holding area.

end of the war the United States Army Air Service brought the idea back to the United States for further investigation and possible development. Assigned to the Experimental Department of the Airplane Engineering Division at McCook Field, Dayton, Ohio, the project was developed. Brought into the project was Dr William Durand from the NACA (National Advisory Committee for Aeronautics) the forerunner of NASA (National Aeronautic and Space Administration), who in turn brought into the team Dr Moss who had been working on a similar theory with General Electric.

The P-38 with superchargers on the production line were the scooters with sidecars used by the workforce to fetch small materials.

Within a year the team had developed a 400-hp Liberty-12 engine that operated successfully at the top of Pike's Peak, Colorado – a height of 14,110 feet. This showed that the supercharger could be used to compensate for the lack of air available to an engine when at high altitude without loss of power or performance.

Over the next few years General Electric developed a series of turbo-superchargers which culminated in the manufacture of the B-model that was fitted into the Allison V-1710 engine that powered the P-38 Lightning.

The problem of compressibility or `Shock Stall' as it was still known was still a cause for concern. The designers and engineers agreed that if they

P-38E outdoor production line in 1941.

couldn't control it they would at least stay away from it. The answer was to install dive brakes. So as not to halt the now flowing production line, it was decided that the dive brakes would be an add-on item. They took the shape of two accordion-type flaps that were attached to the main wing spar, just below each engine boom, with thirty percent of the chord behind the wing's leading edge. Controlled by a trigger on the control wheel, the dive brakes were activated electrically and when not in use were retracted flush into the underside of the wing. Although the aircraft could still run into trouble with compressibility if the angle of dive exceeded 60 degrees, the dive brakes were very effective. Despite the modification being tested and approved by February 1943, it wasn't until April 1944 that the modification was introduced into the construction of the P-38J-25 model.

CHAPTER TWO

'...those aircraft will be fighting within thirty-six hours of leaving here.'

The arrival of the P-38F into squadron service boosted the firepower for the USAAF considerably. A total of 527 P-38Fs were built, 377 were ordered by the USAAF and 150 by the Royal Air Force. Only three of the aircraft ever reached the RAF, the remaining 147 were absorbed into the USAAF. There were five models of the P-38F, the P-38F-1 had racks fitted to carry either two fuel drop tanks or two 1,000-lb bombs. The other variations, the P-38-5, -13 and -15 had only minor modifications such as on the -15 additional manoeuvring flaps.

The first Lightning declared to be combat ready, the P-38F-1- LO on its initial test flight.

The first recorded combat incident involving the P-38 Lightning, was in the New Guinea area, when an unarmed P-38F-4, returning from a photo-reconnaissance mission, was attacked by Japanese Zero fighters. Riddled with holes and with one engine crippled, the pilot feathered the dead engine and put his remaining engine on full power. Within minutes, much to the relief of the pilot, and the surprise of the Japanese pilots who had never seen a Lightning before, it quickly left the Zeros in its wake.

Back in the United States, General George Kenney, USAAC, visited the Lockheed plant in California and urged the company to move into 24-hour production on the P-38 Lightning. `Project Snowman' was one of his projects, this was the special conversion for the Lightnings to operate in the inclement weather of the Aleutian Islands. So desperate was he to

Ground crew refuelling an F-5 photo-reconnaissance Lightning in preparation for a test flight from Burbank, California.

get the aircraft, that Kenney, not known for his tact and diplomacy, rasped at Lockheed's President,

> *' Those aircraft will be fighting within thirty-six hours of leaving here, so lets get them out of here.'*

There was another reason for the desperate need for a powerful fighter, and that was that the Japanese had managed to get a foothold in the Aleutian Islands, which in effect they had landed on American territory and set up bases there. The Japanese Army had landed more than 4,000 soldiers on the islands of Attu and Kiska in an attempt to draw the US Navy into the area. This trap, had Admiral Nimitz taken the bait, would have left the Pacific Theatre of war to the mercy of the Japanese Fleet. As matters turned out Admiral Nimitz declined the offer and instead thrashed the Japanese Fleet at Midway. This of course left Japanese soldiers firmly entrenched in the Aleutian Islands and a potential threat to the North American continent and Alaska.

P-38Es of the 54th Fighter Squadron, 343rd Fighter Group, US 11th Air Force at Longview Field on Adak Island in the Aleutians.

The biggest threat to both sides in the Aleutian Islands was the weather, which at its best was inclement. At the beginning of the war the 11th and 18th Fighter Squadrons, flying P-39s and P-40s, had been assigned to Alaska, but it was soon realised that they did not have the range to patrol the 1,200 mile Aleutian Archipelago. They had, however, seen some action when Japanese carrier based aircraft attacked the US Naval base at Dutch Harbour. Two P-40s flying from their base at Otter Point on the island of Umnak, which was 80 miles from Dutch Harbour, shot down two Nakajima Ki-43 Hayabusa (Peregrine Falcon) fighters.

The answer was the P-38 Lightning and in the summer of 1942 a number of these aircraft were assigned to the 54th Fighter Squadron. One of the new assignments given to the Lightnings, was to attack the Japanese on the island of Kiska. Attempts had been made before but the aircraft had to turn back because of lack of fuel, this time, however, the P-38 Lightning was capable of making the trip and back. The first offensive mission was carried out on 3 September when two P-38 Lightnings, flown by Lieutenants Victor Walton and George Laven, attacked the shipping and flying boats in the harbour at Attu. Both aircraft returned safely.

P-38F Lightning `Elsie' of the 431st Fighter Squadron, 475th Fighter Group, US 5th Air Force after its nosewheel collapsed on landing.

The atrocious weather conditions in the Aleutians claimed more pilots than the Japanese did. This was highlighted during an escort mission when four P-38 Lightnings were escorting a B-17 bomber to a new airstrip on the island of Adak, 375 miles west of Umnak. Because the fog was so bad, the aircraft were flying about ten feet above the water and the number one aircraft could not see numbers three and four, the visibility was that bad. When the formation reached the landing strip it was realised that numbers three and four were not with them. It was discovered later that they had run into a rock sticking out of the water and were killed. It was also a fact that if a pilot had to ditch in the waters off the Aleutian islands, the chances of surviving the icy cold water was measured in minutes and very few did survive.

By September 1942 there were three fighter squadrons based in the Aleutian Islands, the 11th, 18th and 54th and were formed into the 343rd Fighter Group of the US 11th Air Force. Throughout the winter and following spring, the Group pounded the Japanese positions on Attu and Kiska relentlessly. Then on 11 May the US Army's Seventh Division went ashore at Attu, supported by the P-38 Lightnings of the 343rd Fighter Group and after seven weeks of intensive fighting overwhelmed the Japanese force of 2,500 men.

Comforting sight for American troop on the Philippine Islands as an F-5A photo-reconnaissance Lightning flies overhead.

After securing the island of Attu, the American Army looked at recapturing the last Japanese held island of Kiska. Two months after they had recaptured Attu, the American Seventh Division went ashore on the island of Kiska, only to find that the remnants of the entire Japanese garrison had been spirited away under the cover of dense fog by the Japanese navy. A quite remarkable feat.

When General Carl Spatz was demanding faster and better aircraft for the North Africa campaign, he asked for the P-38 Lightning. When told the aircraft was a good fast-flying gun platform but there were reservations about its ability to survive high speed dives, he replied,

' I'd rather have an airplane that goes like hell and has a few things wrong with it, than one that won't go like hell and has a few things wrong with it.'

He got his aircraft.

It has to be remembered that at this point in time the United States of America was not in the war, although the military hierarchy realised that sooner or later they would become involved, so preparations had to be made. The problem of getting aircraft across the Atlantic Ocean was a cause of great concern to the Americans. Getting the big four-engined bombers and transport aircraft across was not a problem, British and Canadian ferry pilots had been doing this since the outbreak of the war. It was the smaller aircraft that was the worry. Putting them on freighters and cargo ships and ferrying them across in large convoys, was one

One of the first P-38 Lightnings to arrive in Britain after flying across the Atlantic via Greenland.

solution, but this took time and in the early part of the war the German U-boat wolf packs were having a field day with the convoys. It was decided that if airstrips were created on Greenland and Iceland, a stepping-stone system would be a viable alternative.

In July 1941, just before America was forced into the war, a base was set up in Iceland by US Marines supported by P-40 aircraft from the 33rd Pursuit Squadron of the 8th Pursuit Group. The aircraft had arrived aboard the aircraft carrier USS *Wasp* and had flown off the deck to land at the base. (In May 1942 pursuit groups were re-designated fighter groups and pursuit squadrons - fighter squadrons). By the end of the year 882 aircraft out of a total of 950, had been safely delivered across the ocean by means of the stepping-stone airfields. They consisted of 366 heavy bombers, 150 medium bombers, 183 transports and 178 P-38 Lightnings belonging to the 1st and 14th Fighter Groups. There were some inevitable casualties and of the 950 aircraft that left America 68 were lost.

Then on 27 June 1942, 80 P-38 Lightnings of the 37th, 71st and 94th Fighter Squadrons, 1st Fighter Group, departed from Bangor, Maine, together with 20 B-17Es from the 341st. Bombing Squadron, 97th Bomber Group. By now two additional airfield in Greenland, Blue West One and Blue West Eight, had been set up and both airfields were equipped with radio navigational aids. Two of the five plane flights that made the crossing ran into trouble, when the weather closed in on them. All the airfields within the vicinity were shut down because of bad weather, so the two flights, now very low on fuel, chose to make an emergency landing on the ice cap.

The first P-38 Lightning attempted a wheels down landing, but lost its undercarriage on the rough icy terrain. The remaining Lightnings and the B-17 went in one after another with their wheels up. All the aircraft got down safely and no one was injured. The crews were found a couple of days later by the crew of a B-24 Liberator and were rescued by dog-sled teams. The location of the aircraft was given as 65 º 20 'N; 45 º 20 'W. In 1980 the aircraft were discovered in the ice and in the 1990's some of the aircraft were recovered from below the ice and found to be in remarkable condition. The incident later became the subject of a book named the `The Lost Squadron'.

However, there were aircraft that just simply disappeared. In one incident 16 Lightnings of the 50th Fighter Squadron led by four B-17 bombers, left Goose Bay, Labrador, on 1 August 1943 heading for Greenland. While over the Davis Strait, one of the Lightnings, flown by Lieutenant Goodrich, just simply disappeared even though they were all in visual contact with each other and flying above a 7,000 feet overcast. Within minutes his disappearance had been noted and one of the B-17s dropped below the overcast and carried out a search pattern. The seas below were extremely rough and the visibility below the 600 feet ceiling left a lot to be desired. After 45 minutes of circling the area, the B-17 climbed back through the overcast and returned to join the remainder of the group. Lieutenant Goodrich and his aircraft were never found.

P-38F fitted with Skis.

A number of fighter squadrons on route across the Atlantic invariably stayed on the Icelandic bases to aid the 33rd Fighter Group based there and give some additional protection to the defence of these bases. It was during one of these visits by the 37th Fighter Squadron that the first encounter with the German Air Force was experienced. The 37th had arrived on 6 July 1943 and were assigned to remain there until 28 August, when they would be replaced by the 50th Fighter Squadron.

One of the first combat experiences of the P-38 Lightning was on 15 August 1942, when P-38s attached to the 54th Fighter Squadron at Adak in the Aleutian Islands, flying patrols from Umnak along the Aleutian chain of islands. The Lightnings came across two Japanese Kawanishi H8K3 four-engined flying boats, who were carrying out a photo-reconnaissance mission on the American bases and shot them down. Ten

Colonel Leon Gray, USAAF, inspecting the damage to the tail fin of his F-5A (P-38) photo-reconnaissance Lightning after being hit by a 20-mm shell during a mission.

days later a P-38D of the 37th. Fighter Squadron flown by Lieutenant Elza E. Shahan was on patrol off Iceland, when he spotted a Focke-Wulf Fw200C-4/U-1 *Kurier* being attacked by a Bell P-39 Airacobra from the 33rd. Fighter Squadron, flown by Lieutenant Joseph Shaffer, of the Iceland Base Command. One of the Focke-Wulf's four engines burst into flames, but within minutes it had been extinguished. With his guns empty, Shaffer could only watch helplessly as the Fw200C continued on its way. But then Lieutenant Elza Shahan manoeuvred his Lightning into position and opened fire with all his guns. Seconds later the large reconnaissance Fw200C exploded and the flaming wreckage plunged headlong into the icy waters below. This was the first German aircraft to be shot down by the USAAF in the European Theatre of Operations (ETO) of World War Two.

With this victory under its belt, the 37th Fighter Squadron, replaced by the 50th Fighter Squadron, continued onto England to join up with its sister units the 48th and 49th Fighter Squadrons which together made up 14th Fighter Group. On 24 April 1943 two P-38 Lightnings, flown by Lieutenants Harry Stengle and James McNulty from the 50th, jumped a Junkers Ju88 on a reconnaissance flight over Iceland and shot it down.

Two Lightning fighter groups arrived in England, the 1st and 14th Fighter Groups belonging to the US 8th Air Force. The 1st Fighter Group was based at Ibsley, Hampshire, the 14th at Atcham, Shrewsbury. It had been intended for them to support the B-17 bombers as they made their almost daily bombing runs over Germany in preparation for an attack on Europe by the Allies. Both Roosevelt and Churchill agreed that an assault on Europe was out of the question before the Spring of 1944, so it was decided to proceed with `Operation *Torch*', the invasion of North Africa. This resulted in the formation of the US 12th Air Force and all the P-38 units in England were to be assigned to it. In the meantime the Groups carried out practice sweeps over the English Channel with RAF fighter squadrons and carried out simulated attacks on bomber squadrons. This preparation work helped the Americans to familiarise themselves with British radio procedures and obtain intelligence information.

Then on 24 October 1943 the Groups were alerted to the fact that they were on the move. Rumour was rife but no one knew where they were going. The ground crews were shipped out on ships from Liverpool and all the P-38 Lightnings flown to Land's End, Cornwall. On 8 November the aircraft took off to fly to Gibraltar, `Operation *Torch*' had begun.

Another fighter group arrived in England in September 1943 the 55th Fighter Group, consisting of the 38th, 338th and 343rd Fighter Squadrons.

David Douglas Duncan inside a special capsule beneath the port wing of a P-38 Lightning from which he took many battlefield photographs.

Based at Nuthampstead, Hertfordshire, the group was fully operational within six weeks of arriving. The arrival of the Lightning squadrons was of immense relief to the bomber crews of the US 8th Air Force. Up to this point in time they had been escorted part of the way to their targets by P-47 Thunderbolts. At the borders with Germany the fighter escort had to leave because they had insufficient fuel to continue, leaving the bomber crews exposed to the packs of Me 109s that descended upon them. This was highlighted on the day before the US 55th Fighter Group became operational – 17 August 1943. This was the day when 230 Boeing B-17 Flying Fortresses of the US 8th Bomber Command, escorted by P-47 Thunderbolts, took off from England to raid the ball-bearing works at Schweinfurt. Sixty B-17 Flying Fortresses and their crews were lost on the raid. The need for long-range escort fighters was never so great.

With the arrival of the P-38 Lightning the long-range bombers would have an escort of P-47 Thunderbolts or Spitfires and when at the end of

P-38 Lightnings being towed along Queens Drive, Liverpool toward Liverpool aerodrome in the early morning mist.

P-38H being serviced at Bassingbourne, England whilst waiting to accompany the bombers on a raid.

their safe operating range, would be replaced by the P-38 Lightning. The Lightning would then escort the bombers into enemy held territory and protect them throughout the raid. On their return, P-47 Thunderbolts would meet them and escort them back to their base. Bombing missions were taking place night and day, the Royal Air Force Bomber Command carrying out night raids, whilst the United States Army Air Force carried out daylight ones.

The main escort fighters came from the P-38 Lightnings of the 55th Fighter Group supplemented by Lightnings from the 20th Fighter Group. Raids on Bremen, Münster and Solingen at the beginning of November 1943, accounted for the loss of 17 P-38 Lightnings whilst the Luftwaffe lost 18 fighters. During one raid on Bremen on 29 November the 55th Fighter Group lost seven Lightnings for seven enemy fighters claimed. The reputation of the Lightning was becoming its greatest weapon, as was apparent on 5 December when long-range bombers carried out a raid on Solingen on the Ruhr. P-47 Thunderbolts escorted the B-17s part of the way and picked them up on their way back, whilst P-38 Lightnings escorted the bombers over the target area. Whilst under the protection of the Lightnings not one of the bombers was attacked.

A P-38H Lightning of the 20th Fighter Group being prepared for a mission at Kingscliffe.

A P-38H of 38th FS, 55th Fighter Group after coming to grief in landing at Marston. Foam on the starboard engine shows that an engine fire may have occured just afterwards.

The *Luftwaffe*, now extremely wary of the P-38 Lightning, would track the bombers and their escorts and use what appeared to be a lone fighter tracking them whilst other German fighters patrolled just out of sight. The idea was to try and attract the escorting Lightnings to leave their charges and go after the `sitter', as it was called, and draw them into a

P-38F Lightnings on patrol. All these aircraft were flown by sergeant-pilots who were known as General Arnold's `White-Haired Boys'.

trap thus reducing the fighter cover. On a couple of occasions the trap worked but the Allies soon got wise and ignored the `sitter'.

On the other side of the world in the South Pacific the P-38 Lightning was beginning to `introduce' itself to the Japanese fighters. Up to this point the Japanese fighter pilots had to contend with the US Navy and Marine F4F Wildcats as an opponent and although as tough and worthy an opponent as any fighter aircraft could be, when the improved version of the Zero came along they started to struggle. Supported by the Bell P-400 fighter (this was the British export model of the P-39 of which a large number were intercepted when America entered the war), the appearance of the P-38 quickly evened up the odds. The role of the P-38 was as a ground attack

The P-38F Lightning at Guadalcanal about to take off on escort duties.

fighter, whilst the P-400, after having no success as a high-altitude fighter, was used for low-level strafing and bombing attacks against Japanese airfields. The tide was starting to change in favour of the Allies.

After the Japanese attack on the naval base at Pearl Harbor on 7 December 1941 their armies moved swiftly, and almost unopposed, through the Far East. Within months they controlled Burma, Thailand, Malaya, French Indochina, part of New Guinea, Solomon Islands, New Britain and the Philippines. Information on their troop movements were desperately needed, so four F-4, the photographic version of the P-38E Lightning, were assigned to the 8th Photographic Squadron based in

P-38F with a photographic capsule mounted beneath the inner port wing. The wartime photographer D D Duncan was inside this capsule taking photographs of the war. Okinawa, 1945

Melbourne, Australia, on 7 April 1942. The squadron was under the command of Major Karl Polifka and by the middle of July the squadron, having moved to Port Moresby, New Guinea, became fully operational.

The Japanese forces who were entrenched on the surrounding islands, were now starting to feel the full weight of the Allied advances. The Battle of the Coral Sea in May, followed by the Battle of Midway in the June, had cost the Japanese Navy dear and had reduced their fleet considerably. It was only a question of time before the Allied armies started to regain their lost territories. General MacArthur and Admiral

F-5E of the 28th Photographic Reconnaissance Squadron about to touch down on Yontan airstrip, Okinawa, Japan.

Nimitz needed information on the Japanese positions and troop movements and to do this the US 8th Photographic Squadron `mapped' a major part of eastern New Guinea and New Britain.

The greatest threat to the unarmed Lightnings of the 8th was the weather. The P-38 could outrun anything that the Japanese had in the air and could climb higher. The fact that they carried no weapons was a cause for some frustration for some of the pilots, no more so than when Lieutenant Alex Guerry came upon four `Rufe' (Nakajima A6M2-N Navy Type 2) fighter seaplanes whilst making a low photographic pass. Frustrated at not being able to attack them in the conventional manner, Lt Guerry started to make very low passes on the enemy aircraft, eventually forcing them to put down on the water. As the last one settled, Guerry made an exceptionally low pass and flipped the seaplane over on

P-38Fs of No. 347 Fighter Group on Guadacanal.

to its back with his propeller wash. He even took a photograph of the aircraft on the water to substantiate his claim.

This wasn't the only incident of an enemy aircraft being destroyed without actually being shot down. During an attack on the Japanese base on the island of Lae, Lieutenant Robert Faurot of 39th Fighter Squadron at Port Moresby aimed his bomb at the runway but missed. The bomb struck the water at the end of the runway and exploded in front of a Zero that was just getting airborne. The Japanese aircraft flew into the enormous column of water created by the explosion and crashed.

The first fully combat ready P-38F-1 Lightnings arrived in Brisbane, in Australia, at the beginning of August 1942, but because of a number of

P-38F on Guadacanal.

problems with the aircraft, such as faulty inverters, missing ammunition feeds and leaking fuel tanks, it was November before they were ready to go into combat. At the end of November the whole squadron was moved

P-38F over Guadacanal.

to Laloki in preparation for the big push.

A number of other squadron were now beginning to receive the P-38 Lightnings and among them was the 339th Fighter Squadron belonging to 347th Fighter Group based on Henderson Field, Guadalcanal, Solomon Islands. Their first mission was to fly as escort to five B-17 bombers of the 11th Bomber Group on an attack on an enemy convoy.

The first recorded successes against the Japanese fighters was on 27

December 1942 when 12 P-38 Lightnings of the 39th Fighter Squadron, led by Captain Thomas Lynch, were scrambled from their airfield at Laloki, the 14 Mile Airfield at Port Moresby. Over Dobodura, 125 miles from their base, they intercepted 25-30 enemy fighters and bombers. Within minutes the sky was a whirling mass of hot metal as 12 Lightnings, cannons and guns blazing, attacked the formation. Fifteen Japanese aircraft were shot down in the ensuing mêlée, without the loss of a single American aircraft. The remaining Japanese aircraft high-tailed it out of the area hotly pursued by the Lightnings. The American pilots were soon forced to withdraw because of lack of fuel and ammunition, but the message the Japanese pilots took back to their bases was one of serious concern about this new lethal fighting machine. Among the

America's top ace (40 confirmed victories) Lieutenant Dick Bong, USAAF, in the cockpit of his P-38 Lightning in New Guinea. After the war Dick Bong joined Lockheed as a test pilot but was killed when the P/F-80A Shooting Star he was testing had engine failure at low altitude and crashed.

American pilots was one Lieutenant Richard I Bong, who by the end of the war became the USAAF's top fighter pilot.

American pilots who had flown other model fighters in combat, soon began to realise that the P-38 Lightning had every advantage in the fighter pilot's book except a sharp turning radius and a steep climb. They had flown against the superior Zero fighter and had learned lessons the hard way, now this time, using their experience and with a superior fighter aircraft, they were ahead of the game. The success ratio changed dramatically from 2-1 to 20-1.

As the Japanese Zero improved so did the P-38. The arrival of the P-38G model fitted with the new F.10 engines enabled the aircraft to cruise continuously with a rating of 1,100-hp per engine. The first of the G-models, the P-38G-5-LO were fitted with the new B-13 turbo-

Lieutenant S Ford, USAAC, walking away in a state of shock after his P-38 Lightning was shot down by a Japanese Zero. He was unharmed, testimony to the rugged construction of the P-38 Lightning but as can be seen the aircraft is a total wreck.

superchargers, had a new oxygen system and the new SCR-247N radio system. A total of 1,082 G-models were built, the majority of which were converted and assigned to photo-reconnaissance squadrons. A few of them were modified to carry a 2,000-lb bomb under each wing and one was modified to carry a streamlined tank that had a transparent nose and a hinged aft section. The idea behind the scheme was to carry urgent stretcher cases, one of the tanks was designed to carry two persons, but it was never adopted.

When the 8th Photographic Squadron reported the sighting of a Japanese convoy heading for the Japanese base at Lae, New Guinea, the 9th Fighter Squadron from the 49th Fighter Group had just received their new P-38G Lightnings. Two days later they, and a number of P-40 Curtiss Warhawks attacked the convoy. During the next three days 50 enemy aircraft were destroyed with minimal losses to the Americans. Without doubt the tide was beginning to turn.

CHAPTER THREE

'...destroy Admiral Yamamoto.'

The end of 1942 brought a lull in the fighting, there were skirmishes, but nothing on the scale the previous six months had seen. Then at the beginning of March 1943, P-38 (F-4) Lightnings from 8th Photo-reconnaissance Squadron, sighted eight large Japanese transports accompanied by eight destroyers with the intention, it was discovered later, of landing 6,000 troops on the island of Lae. A full scale attack was planned from the air, consisting of 16 Lightnings from the 9th and 39th Fighter Squadrons, 28 B-17 Flying Fortresses of 5th Air Force, B-25s, A-20s and Australian Beaufighters. Known as the Battle of the Bismark Sea, the bombers and fighter-bombers attacked the convoy, whilst the P-38s covered them and during the next two days shot down nine enemy fighters for the loss of three of their own. Meanwhile the B-17s, B-25 Mitchells, A-20s and Beaufighters carried out skip bombing and strafing runs on the convoy, sinking three transports and two destroyers. Two more of the destroyers were severely damaged as were the remaining five transports, the result being that only four destroyers remained intact and it was they that picked up and rescued 2,800 enemy soldiers from the water and returned them to Rabaul. On the scale of battles it was not huge by other standards, but the effect on the morale of the Japanese navy and army was immense. Suddenly they were not the victorious warriors sweeping across the Pacific carrying all before them, but an army with its back against the wall.

Then on 17 April 1943 the Japanese suffered a huge setback when Admiral Isoroku Yamamoto was killed during an attack by P-38 Lightnings from the 347th Fighter Group. US Naval intelligence had intercepted a message saying that Admiral Yamamoto, Commander-in-Chief of the Imperial Japanese Navy, would be leaving his base on Rabaul for an inspection trip to Ballale, Bougainville. He was to be accompanied by Admiral Matome Ugaki. The two Admirals would be in separate Mitsubishi G4M1 Navy

Captain Lanphier receiving the Distinguished Flying Cross and Silver Star from Brigadier General Dean C Strother for his part in destroying Admiral Yamamoto's mission.

bombers known to the Allies as `Bettys'. They would escorted by six Zero fighters of the 309th *Kokutai*. A blue tissue cablegram, this was used by the Navy for top priority messages, was sent by Secretary of the Navy Knox to the USAAC at Guadalcanal. The reason being that Admiral Yamamoto's itinerary took his aircraft to withing striking distance of the P-38 Lightnings based at Guadalcanal. The message gave the exact times for the take-off and landing of Admiral Yamamoto's aircraft and the last line read:

`Maximum effort should be made to destroy Admiral Yamamoto'.

The message arrived on the desks of Major John W Mitchell and Captain Thomas G Lanphier Jr. Sixteen P-38 Lightnings were assigned to the `assassination', twelve of them would take care of the escorting fighters, whilst the remaining four went after the two `Betty' bombers. Two of the Lightnings aborted the mission with engine trouble soon after they had taken off, this left 10 Lightnings to take care of the escort fighters. The timing of the attack was of paramount importance mainly because the attack would take place on the outer limits of the Lightnings range, thus limiting the time they would have to carry out the attack. The one thing that was in their favour, was that Admiral Yamamoto was a stickler for punctuality to the point of it being almost an obsession.

At 09:43 hours the Japanese formation was spotted and the Lightnings swooped into the attack.

The first wave of American fighters drew the escorting Zeros away from the `Bettys', whilst the second wave attacked then from another angle. This left the way clear for the four remaining Lightnings to go after the `Betty' bombers and the two Admirals.

Lanphier released his belly tanks and prepared to go after the two bombers, then he heard Holmes voice on the R/T saying that he couldn't release his belly tanks. Lanphier looked back over his shoulder and saw Holmes frantically attempting to dislodge his tanks be wriggling his aircraft, but to no avail. Holmes had to break off as the Lightning's speed and manoeuvrability would be reduced substantially and leave him a sitting duck for any Japanese Zero that happened to see him.

The Japanese pilots took their bombers down to treetop level chased by Captain Thomas Lanphier. He sent a long burst of gunfire from his cannons into the side of the fuselage of Yamamoto's aircraft and into the starboard wing. Suddenly flames spurted from the engine followed almost immediately by the starboard wing breaking away. The aircraft rolled on to its port side and plunged into the jungle. The second `Betty' had turned toward the sea flying close to the surface with Lieutenant Rex Barber on its tail. Lt Holmes went after one of the escorting Zeros, whilst Barber fired a long burst into the fuselage and wing of the `Betty' and as he looked back, he saw the `Betty' explode as it hit the surface of the water. Admiral Matome Ugaki somehow managed to survive the crash with just a broken arm and a few bruises and swam ashore. With the loss of Admiral Yamamoto, Japan had lost its top strategist and the loss was felt across the Japanese military hierarchy with great concern. The P-38 Lightning on the other hand had chalked up an impressive victory and by this one act had made a significant contribution to the war in the Pacific.

Admiral Ugaki was to later lose his life when, after the Emperor had given

P-38L in natural finish. Pacific Area.

his surrender broadcast to the Japanese people on 15 August 1945, he climbed aboard a fighter-bomber with two other officers, to carry out a Kamikaze attack on the US Naval base at Okinawa. The aircraft was shot down before it reached the base and the wreckage spread across the beach. Admiral Ugaki's body was found inside the wreckage of the bomber.

Admiral Nimitz's commander in the South Pacific, Vice-Admiral Halsey, together with General MacArthur, took advantage of the turmoil within the Japanese military hierarchy to resume their offensive in an attempt to surround Rabaul. The 347th Fighter Group in the Solomon Islands, was still taking its toll on the enemy fighters, but at a cost. Aircraft that were lost during these skirmishes were not being readily replaced, which meant that the squadron's strength was diminishing almost daily. The Curtiss P-40 Warhawk was then having to take on the burden of attacking the Japanese Zeros and until new aircraft arrived for the US 13th Air Force they would have to manage.

A modified P-38L that carried a bombardier in its nose. The idea was that this aircraft would lead a formation of P-38 Lightnings to a target at which point, on the instructions of the bombardier, they would release their bomb loads. A number of these raids were carried out and with great success. It was a risky position for the bombardier to be in, because if the aircraft was hit the bombardier was unable to get out.

In New Guinea however, the US 5th Air Force, under the command of General Kenney, had acquired 115 new P-38G aircraft and used them to form a new group, the 475th Fighter Group. In June 1943 Major George Prentice, commander of the 39th Fighter Squadron, was chosen as 475th Fighter Group commander and his first job was to select the best pilots and commanders from the 39th and 80th Fighter Squadrons to bolster his new group. The group would consist of the 431st, 432nd and 433rd Fighter

Squadrons and would be equipped with P-38G Lightnings. An additional group, 348th Fighter Group, under the command of Major Neil E Kearby, was added to the 5th Air Force at the same time, but they were equipped with North American P-47 Thunderbolts. The 475th was to later earn the nickname of `Satan's Angels' it was one that the Japanese pilots would attest to.

P-38F Lightning `Elsie' of the 431st Fighter Squadron, 475th Fighter Group, US 5th Air Force after it nosewheel collapsed on landing.

In one incident concerning the 475th Fighter Group, the 432nd Fighter Squadron were supporting an Allied landing with sixteen aircraft, twelve of which were P-38 Lightnings, when ten Japanese bombers and 38 fighters were spotted closing in to attack the invasion force. Four of the Lightnings dived upon the enemy aircraft in a fast attack, causing the Japanese formation to break. As they broke, the remaining eight P-38 Lightnings hit them like runaway locomotives and shot down seven bombers and eleven fighters in a matter of minutes, with the loss of two Lightnings and one pilot. The remaining Japanese bombers and fighters left the scene as fast as they could.

The summer of 1943 was the start of the main offensive against the Japanese on Rabaul and by the beginning of September the Army, under the command of Admiral Halsey, had secured New Georgia. At the same time as Halsey was attacking New Georgia, Australian troops under the overall command of General MacArthur were attacking Salamaua, Lae, and the important airfield at Nadzab. The attacks began on the 17 August with the US 5th Air Force carrying out a five-day intensive attack on the Wewak area having, on the first day, caught the Japanese completely by surprise. Over half of the Japanese aircraft were caught on the ground and destroyed by bombers whilst squadrons of the 475th Fighter Group took care of any that managed to get in the air. Over the next few days they were joined by P-38 Lightnings of the 9th, 39th and 80th Fighter Squadrons, taking out what was left of the Japanese aircraft in the area.

US Marines were now just 300 miles south-east of Rabaul, whilst the Australians were 450 miles south-west of the island. What was becoming

P-38L of the 18th Fighter Group, US 13th Air Force in the SW Pacific Area flying on one engine after being hit by anti- aircraft fire.

P-38 Lightnings of the 39th Fighter Squadron returning to their airfield at Laloki, Port Moresby, New Guinea, at low level after a very successful mission.

apparent was that the Japanese air force in a desperate attempt to stem the tide of the Allied forces, were losing any supremacy that they had in the air. Their aircraft were being systematically destroyed daily with very few losses to the Americans. Such was the speed of the airborne assault, that by the end of September plans were in place for an all-out assault on Rabaul. The US 5th Air Force, together with 13th Air Force, under the command of General Harmon, was moved up to Dobodura in preparation for the attack.

P-38J of the 27th Fighter Squadron, 1st Fighter Group showing the inner wing pylons used to carry rockets.

The offensive against the 100,000 Japanese troops on Rabaul began on 12 October 1943, with a massive bomber raid consisting of 107 Liberators, Mitchells and Beaufighters escorted by 106 P-38 Lightnings from the 5th Air Force. Throughout October and well into November, the raids continued. The bomber groups taking it in turn whilst the Lightnings accompanied every raid offering protection from the now desperate Japanese fighter pilots. Such was the scale of the bombing on Rabaul, that the surrounding islands were taken with little if any resistance and the invasion of Rabaul was cancelled as it was now deemed to be an unnecessary waste of human resources and material. With all their supply lines cut-off, the Japanese were left on Rabaul to determine their own fate.

In North Africa, Operation *Torch* had been launched on 8 November 1942 and had been spearheaded by Allied troops going into north-west Africa at Algiers, Mehedia, Safi, Fedhala and Casablanca in French Morocco. There

B-25 Mitchells attacking Junker Ju 52s who were carrying supplies for Rommel's beleaguered army in North Africa. Notice how low to the surface of the sea the aircraft flew in a desperate unsuccessful attempt to avoid detection. Flying escort for the B-25 bombers were P-38 Lightnings.

was limited resistance from the French Vichy troops but this was quickly dealt with and most of the French Vichy soldiers surrended within hours. Since almost the beginning of the war, the British and Commonwealth troops had been fighting a bitter battle against the German and Italian armies in north-east Africa. As if to herald the launch of Operation *Torch*, Montgomery and the British 8th Army, who had been penned in at El Alamein, Egypt, broke free and started to pursue Field Marshal Rommel's *Afrika Korps* back across the desert into Libya. With the landings in north-west Africa closing in on Rommel's troops from the west and the 8th Army closing from the east, this in effect trapped the *Afrika Korps* in a giant 1,700-mile-across pincer. To bring the *Afrika Korps* to its knees the Allies needed to sever the enemy's supply lines and the easiest way to do that was from the air.

General Montgomery, who had complete faith in his air force commander Air Marshal Tedder, RAF, left the details of this part of the plan to him.

B-17 Flying Fortresses of the 15th Air Force being escorted by P-38 Lightnings who leave their twin vapour trails high in the sky as they weave their protective cover for the bombers.

Tedder commanded the Desert Air Force, which included the US 9th Air Force and controlled the air over north-east Africa. General Dwight Eisenhower, USA, who was in overall command of Operation *Torch*, had very little experience in the use of tactical air power, spread General `Jimmy' Doolittle's US 12th Air Force across 600 miles of desert.

On the day of the invasion, P-38 Lightnings from the 1st and 14th Fighter Group, assigned to the 12th Air Force, left England and flew from Land's End to Gibraltar. On the 11 November the 48th Fighter Squadron from the 14th Air Group, carried out the first mission, a reconnaissance flight. Eight days later the squadron moved to the airfield at Maison Blanche, unaware that the *Luftwaffe* had recently arrived at El Aouina, near Tunis, some days earlier. That night, before the squadron had time to settle to their new surroundings, German bombers, accompanied by fighters, attacked and badly damaged seven P-38 Lightnings in a raid on the airfield. Extensive damage was also caused to the hangars and administrative buildings which incurred a number of casualties.

The attack was not enough to put the Squadron out of action and after acquiring a number of other P-38 Lightnings and pilots from other

P-38 Lightnings of the 15th Air Force heading for home on the completion of the mission.

The P-38H flown by Lockheed test pilot Tony LeVier on its initial test flight.

The P-38H-5 with improved superchargers which gave the aircraft a greater high altitude performance.

squadrons, they carried out their first combat mission two days later, when they escorted 20 C-47s to Constantine. Two days later the airfield was attacked again by Junkers Ju 87s and 88s destroying two P-38 Lightnings, a Beaufighter, a Boeing B-17 bomber and four Spitfires, the latter was a complete photo-reconnaissance squadron. The only good thing was that the 1st Fighter Group had moved to Nouvion the previous day and the day after the raid the 14th Fighter Group's remaining two squadrons moved to Youks les Bains, which was in north-east Algeria. The airfield was situated in a tiny valley of which the 4,500 feet runway stretched almost the entire length. The foothills either side of the valley rose to a height of 4,000 feet. Besides the 14th's aircraft at the airfield there were a number of Douglas DB-7 light-bombers flown by French airmen. The 14th was joined a week later by the 94th Fighter Squadron from the 1st Fighter Group.

The P-38s were now on almost full-time escort duties and during one incident, on 21 November, six P-38 Lightnings of the 48th Fighter Squadron were escorting twelve B-17 Flying Fortresses on a bombing raid to Tunis, when they tangled with four Me 109s. During the ensuing 30 minute dogfight, Lieutenant Carl Williams chased one of the Me 109s and shot it down, scoring the first victory for the Lightnings in Africa. The other three Me 109s beat a hasty retreat leaving the bombers to unload their deadly cargo uninterrupted. The attack wasn't all one sided. One of the Lightnings,

F-4 in North Africa.

flown by Lieutenant Ayers, was badly shot up during the dogfight and although he managed to get his crippled aircraft back to base, Ayers was badly injured as a result of the crash-landing.

The following day the squadrons were airborne once again and were slowly leaving their mark on the enemy. The 48th Fighter Squadron attacked a troop train on one of the days missions, leaving a trail of desolation behind them. Another mission the same day accounted for another train plus four tanks and, on the way back, discovered a Junkers Ju 88 approaching their field. Fortunately two P-38 Lightning, flown by Lieutenants Sorensen and Shipman, were on standby and took off. After a short dogfight the enemy aircraft was shot down, but not before the Junkers had crippled one of Shipman's engines, forcing him to break off the attack and return to the field.

North Africa conjured up visions of hot sun and deserts to the strategic planners. They had anticipated taking Algeria and the surrounding areas with a degree of ease. This was not to be the case as they had

P-38F of the 94th Fighter Squadron in North Africa.

underestimated the German response and the fact that when the rains came the airfields became seas of mud. During December 1942 missions were cancelled one after another as the big P-38 Lightnings could not be moved through the morass of mud. At one of the airfields, Youks, a solid rock formation that was almost 1,700 feet long and rose gradually into the hills, was discovered adjacent to the existing runway. Manoeuvring one of the P-38s into position, the pilot, Lieutenant Ervin Ethell, taxied his aircraft to the top end of the runway and took off down hill. Seconds later he was airborne and minutes later he landed back on the rock runway facing up-hill, the gradient helping to slow the aircraft down. The airfield at Youks was now an all-weather operational station.

The role of the P-38 Lightnings at Youks was that of a close air support for the US 1st Armoured Division and the British 78th Division. On one of the missions, four Lightnings from the 48th and 49th Fighter Squadrons were carrying out a low-level reconnaissance sortie, when they came upon a

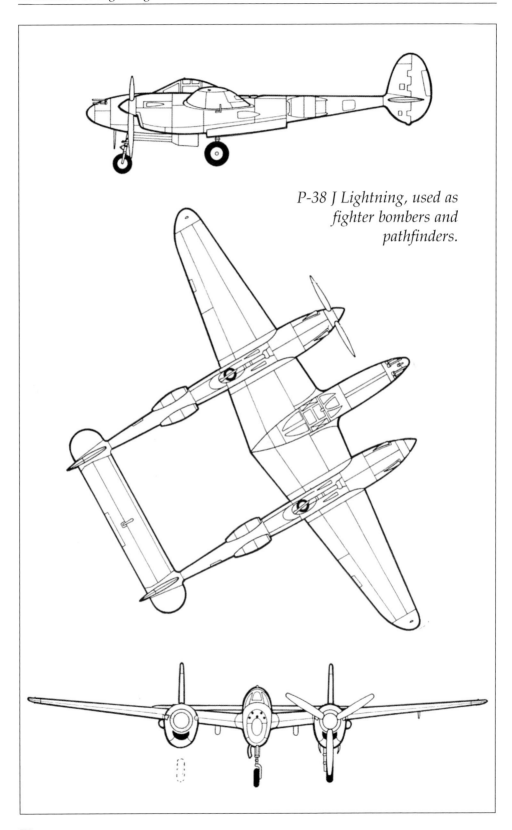

P-38 J Lightning, used as fighter bombers and pathfinders.

formation of between fifteen and twenty Junker Ju 52s escorted by four Messerschmitt Me 109s. Before the Germans could realise what was happening, the four Lightnings swooped down and within minutes had accounted for six Ju 52s and one Me 109. Unfortunately one of the Lightnings was also hit and crashed. Low on fuel and ammunition, the three remaining Lightnings broke off the engagement and headed back to base hugging the ground all the way.

The re-occurring problem of lack of pilots and aircraft raised its head once

P-38J of the 27th Fighter Squadron, 1st Fighter Group, in Italy.

again. So bad was it becoming, that two-aircraft reconnaissance missions were becoming the norm and protecting a bomber group on a mission was to use almost every available aircraft. By the middle of January 1943 the 1st, 4th and 82nd Fighter Groups had less than 90 aircraft between them, where they should have had around 100 *each*. In an effort to boost the supply of aircraft and pilots to the North African campaign, 50 P-38 Lightnings flew via the South Atlantic to North Africa. It highlighted the extent of the P-38's aircraft's range.

One prize the Germans would like to have had, was Colonel Elliot Roosevelt, the son of the President of the United States. Elliot Roosevelt was commander of the 3rd Photo-reconnaissance Group at La Senia, Algeria, which on the face of it was a soft option, but in reality was one of the most

P-38H at Camp Tripoli, Iceland.

A P-38J-5-LO bristling with cannon and machine guns together with the unarmed photo-reconnaissance version the F-5B-1-LO.

dangerous flying jobs in the Air Corps. Photo-reconnaissance aircraft were unarmed and nearly always flew alone. In the event of them being shot down, there was very little chance of anyone knowing where they were, or even if they were alive. Their contribution to the war was equal importance as that of the bombers and fighters that most of the attention was focused upon, but never seemed to receive the recognition they deserved.

The arrival of General Carl Spaatz in North Africa resulted in the creation of the north-west African Air Force (NAAF). General Spaatz had been sent to North Africa by General Eisenhower who had become concerned with the

P-38F (No. 64) in North Africa where the first large scale use was made of the aircraft and it gained its reputation as The Fork-tailed Devil.

way the Air Corps was going, it seemed to him that it was becoming unstructured and consisting of little enclaves. Given a free hand by Eisenhower, General Spaatz brought the chain of command into line with that of the Royal Air Force and in February 1943, integrated it into the Mediterranean Air Command under the command of Air Chief Marshal

Tedder, RAF. The Mediterranean Air Command included the US 9th Air Force and Commonwealth Desert Air Forces under Air Vice-Marshal Conningham. The Allied Air Forces in the desert were now operating as a unit and as one senior officer put it, `We are all now singing from the same hymn sheet'.

The 14th Fighter Group were taken out of combat duties on 29 January 1943. In the short period of time that they had been in action they had lost 32 pilots, 23 of them in aerial combat, the remainder in accidents. They were

P-38 Lightning in its dispersal point being prepared for a mission.

credited with the shooting down of 62 enemy aircraft, seven probables and seventeen damaged, not bad for an outfit that had only been in action for three months.

The P-38 Lightning also commanded a great deal of respect from the pilots of the *Luftwaffe.* One of the pilots, *Leutnant* Johann Pichler of *Jagdgeschwader 77* wrote in his diary:

> *Over Tunisia, my flight encountered four P-38s and we slipped behind them, virtually unnoticed. Although our Gustavs (Me 109Gs) gave all they could, the distance between us and the Lightnings hardly diminished. At a distance of about 500 meters, I fired all my guns, but my shells exploded behind one of the P-38s. After several more ineffective bursts, the US pilots obviously sensed danger. Applying full war-emergency power, they disappeared, leaving us with our mouths wide open. The five- minute chase caused my engine to seize. One of the connecting rods pushed itself right through the cowling...*

Pichler went on to describe his first aerial battles with the P-38 Lightning:

> *In my estimation, the P-38 was more manoeuvrable and faster than our Bf-109G-6, especially since the latter was equipped with two cm (20-mm) underwing gondola weapons. I had never been keen on dogfights with the P-38, but I did manage to shoot down three of them plus four or five B-25 Mitchells. An excellent method of breaking combat was to go into a power dive from high altitude. The P-38 pilots rarely followed us. At first this was unexplainable to us but the mystery cleared up when a captured P-38 pilot told us their ships became too fast to be pulled-out of a dive efficiently.*

Leutnant Pilcher was one of Germany's top aces at the time and had been transferred to North Africa in October 1942. This was the first, but not the last, time he had encountered the P-38 Lightning which left a lasting impression on him. Johann Pilcher finished the war with 52 victories to his credit.

There was one remarkable escape story concerning a pilot from the 14th Fighter Group. In one extremely busy period between the 9 January and 28 January, the group flew 23 missions (232 sorties) and on one of these all six P-38 Lightnings were shot down. One of the pilots, Lieutenant Mark Shipman, managed to crash-land his badly damaged aircraft in the desert near Gafsa. The Arabs in the area, who were not exactly friendly toward the Allies, stripped him of some of his clothes and other belongings, leaving him just in his trousers and boots. He managed to walk back to the nearest base Berteaux, a distance of 250 miles, and at one point strolling through an

Italian Army encampment where he managed to acquire a coat.

The war in the desert had reached a crucial point. The *Afrika Korps* was in retreat and the Allies were closing them up in a pincer movement rapidly. But *Feldmarschall* Erwin Rommel was not known as the `Desert Fox' for nothing. He had plans for a counter-attack, but this relied heavily on aerial supplies of ammunition and food, etc. Over 500 German transport aircraft were made available to him, bringing in supplies from bases in Italy and Sicily. From December 1942 to March 1943 the Germans carried over 40,000 men and 14,000 tons of supplies to the beleaguered *Afrika Korps*.

The Mediterranean Air Command were well aware of what was going on and created `Operation *Flax'* which was carry to out co-ordinated raids against the German transport aircraft and their bases. On the 5 April 1943 the first of these raids took place when 26 P-38 Lightnings of the 1st Fighter

Close-up of the nose section of a F-5G showing the camera ports. Marakesh.

Group made an early morning sweep of the Mediterranean sea, north of the Cape Bone-Bizerte area. The squadron came across over 60 Junker Ju 52s and their fighter escorts consisting of Me 109s, Me 110s, Ju 87s, an Me 210 and a Focke-Wulf Fw 190. The squadron went into the attack and accounted for eleven Ju 52s, three Me 109s and two Ju 87s with the loss of two P-38s. The remaining German aircraft turned and headed back to their base. Whilst this attack was going on, B-25 Mitchell bombers, escorted by a number of P-38 Lightnings of the 95th Fighter Squadron from the 82nd Fighter Group, pounded the Bo Rimoz airfield in Sicily. At the same time other P-38 Lightnings from the 95th Fighter Squadron, escorted a squadron of B-25 Mitchells whilst they combed the Sicilian Straits looking for enemy shipping.

One of the most vicious aerial battles during this period, happened when twenty P-38 Lightnings from the 27th Fighter Squadron, 1st Fighter Group, together with Lightnings from the 71st Fighter Squadron, were escorting twenty B-25 Mitchell bombers. They came across a large formation of between 50 and 60 Ju 52 transports escorted by fifteen Macchi C200 and Fw 190s. With the 71st Fighter Squadron flying top cover the Lightnings from 27th Fighter Squadron swept into the attack. Twenty-eight enemy aircraft were shot down without a single loss to the Americans. It has to be said that

Fuel tank and 1,000-lb bomb slung under the wings of a P-38. This Lightning was one of twenty that attacked the oil refineries at Ploesti, Rumania.

it would appear that all these attacks were carried out by P-38 Lightnings, this is not quite true as they were accompanied on many of these sorties by P-40 Warhawks, who also accounted for some of the German transports and escorts.

Operation *Flax* was a complete success. Control of the air over North Africa was in the hands of the Allies who then shut off all supply lines to the *Afrika Korps*. On 13 May 1943, 270,000 German and Italian soldiers, who had been trapped on the Tunisian coast for months, surrendered and took no more part in the war. This then of course left the Allies with the problem of what to do with them – but then that is another story.

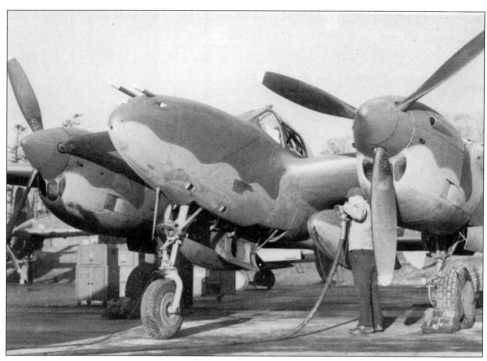

P-38 Lightning having its auxiliary fuel tanks topped up prior to being delivered to its new squadron.

P-38 Lightning with triangular full rocket launchers beneath each wing about to take off on a test-firing flight.

CHAPTER FOUR

'...Mein Gott let this soon be over.'

With the war in North Africa over, attention turned to Sicily and Italy. Again like North Africa, what was needed was for the Allies to take control of the skies and cut off all supply lines to the Axis powers. The date set for the invasion of Sicily, codenamed Operation *Husky*, was set for 10 July 1943. At the beginning of June, fighters and bombers from the Mediterranean Air Command commenced air attacks against German and Italian airfields. That month they destroyed over 1,000 aircraft and had forced the German and Italian Air Forces back into Italy. When 160,000 soldiers from the British 8th Army and US 7th Army landed in Sicily they met with virtually no opposition. If the Allies had thought that because they encountered little or no opposition in Sicily, they were going to push into Italy with the same ease, they were to be very much mistaken. Although the Italians had lost the will to continue fighting, 26 divisions of German infantry had not and they dug their heels in.

The 1st, 14th and 82nd Fighter Groups, together with the 3rd Photo-reconnaissance Group, Squadron RAF and the French Groupe de Reconnaissance 2/33, based in Tunisia, made up the Mediterranean Allied Photo-reconnaissance Wing under the command of Colonel Karl Polifka, USAAF, who took over from Colonel Elliot Roosevelt. Among the pilots was the famed French author, inventor and raconteur Antoine de Saint-Exupéry who at the age of 45 was one of the oldest pilots flying in the wing. Unfortunately de Saint-Exupéry was lost when he failed to return from a photo-reconnaissance mission.

The risks attached to flying unarmed photo-reconnaissance missions was never made more apparent than when Colonel Frank Dunn, USAAF, returning from a mission, dived through a low overcast and found himself approaching a circuit of enemy bombers over their airfield near Cagliri.

Antoine de Saint-Exupéry – Author – Philosopher – Inventor Adventurer and P-38 Lightning pilot in the cockpit of his photo-reconnaissance aircraft.

Joining the circuit, Dunn glanced at the enemy aircraft who in turn looked at him in total disbelief, but fortunately, so surprised, never fired on him. Seizing the moment Dunn saw his chance, and opening up both his engines sped from the area. Flying over the town of Cagliri, Dunn spotted a train pulling into the station but unable to attack the train, he dropped his jettisonable fuel tanks in a last act of defiance. As he turned away he saw them strike the roofs of the carriages. Swinging round for a second look, he was delighted to see enemy troops spilling out of the carriages and running for their lives. This was one of the more lighter and rarer moments that these pilots experienced, the vast majority of the time they lived their lives on a

F-5E Photo-reconnaissance version of the P-38 Lightning in Italy.

knife-edge.

The P-38 fighters on the other hand were in a position to defend themselves and others. With the Italian military almost out of the war, the Allies started to push farther and farther inland. On 14 August the US 12th Air Force launched a massive bomber raid on the railway marshalling yards at Littoria and Lorenzo, near Naples. The force, consisting of 106 Boeing B-17 Flying Fortresses, 106 Martin B-26 Marauders and 66 North American B-

Home of the 3rd Photographic Group which consisted of the 5th, 12th and 23rd Photographic Squadrons in Florence, Italy. The field belonged to the 15 Air Force.

25 Mitchells, was escorted by 90 P-38G-10 and G-15 Lightnings. As they approached the marshalling yards they were attacked by 75 enemy fighters, but the force closed ranks with the result that more than five enemy fighters were destroyed for the loss of only two B-26 Marauders. Extensive damage was caused to the railway marshalling yards putting the German and Italian supply lines under further pressure.

Throughout August 1943 the three P-38 Lightning Groups carried extensive raids on the German retreating positions, strafing trains, convoys, destroying railway tracks and bridges. At the end of August the 1st and 82nd Fighter Groups were ordered to carry out combined and concerted raids against every airfield in Foggia. At 0700 hours on the morning of 25 August, both groups took off and headed inland. Hugging the deck the P-38 Lightnings cut a swathe across the various airfields. Although initially they had the element of surprise, they met with strong opposition from the Germans and Italians, but two hours later the P-38 Lightnings left the area and in their wake more than two hundred enemy aircraft were either badly damaged or destroyed with the loss of just two Lightnings.

A 500-lb. bomb being winched into position beneath the port wing of a P-38 Lightning belonging to the 94th Fighter Squadron at Foggia, Italy

But if this gives the impression that it was all one way traffic, it wasn't. On every raid the Allied fighters and bombers met with stiff opposition and one raid in particular, on the 2 September and the day before General Montgomery made his big push across the Strait of Messina into Italy, 80 P-38G Lightnings from the 82nd Fighter Group escorted a similar number of B-25 Mitchells for a raid on the Cancellor railway marshalling yards north of Naples. They were met with a combined force of German and Italian fighters consisting of Italian Reggiane 2001s, Macchi 202s and German Messerschmitt Bf 109s. As the two forces converged there were over 200 aircraft in the air, 145 of which were fighters and every one fighting for every inch of space. The P-38 Lightnings dropped their auxiliary fuel tanks

Captain John S Litchfield with his crew chief T/Sgt Robert Elkins beside their P-38 Lightning `Sweet Pea' in Italy, 1944.

and plunged headlong into the fray most of which was fought at sea level. At the end of the battle, not one of the B-25 Mitchells were lost, although 10 P-38s were. The enemy however suffered the loss of sixteen Messerschmitt Bf 109s, one Focke-Wulf Fw 190, five Macchi C202s and one Reggiane 2001. A further twelve Me 109s were damaged and had to limp home.

On 3 September 1943 Montgomery's army crossed the Strait of Messina and were soon ashore in Southern Italy. This threat to Italy emboldened King Umberto to demand the resignation of Mussolini and enter into secret negotiations with the Allies in an effort to bring Italy out of the war. On 8 September General Eisenhower announced the surrender of Italian forces. The same day the US 5th Army went ashore at Salerno and the push into Italy began.

Never had the fighting been so fierce, but, if it were possible, it became more intense, when General Mark Clark's US 5th Army carried out an assault on the beaches at Salerno on 9 September as the *Luftwaffe* attacked with in

Group of P-38 pilots having just returned from a fighter sweep over Sicily in which they accounted for ten enemy aircraft. L-R: 1st Lieutenant William Sloan; Flying Officer Frank Hurlbut; 1st Lieutenant Edward Waters; 1st Lieutenant Lawrence Liebers; 2nd Lieutenant L D Jones and 2nd Lieutenant Ward Kuentzel.

excess of 100 aircraft at a time. So fierce were the *Luftwaffe* attacks that for a week the troops were pinned down on the beachheads and the assault almost turned into a retreat. Almost every Allied aircraft in the vicinity was brought into the fray; P-38 Lightnings, A-36 (Dive-bomb) Mustangs, sixteen Squadrons of RAF Spitfires, including one group of American Spitfires. Almost continuously they carried out attacks on the German and Italian airfields and by the 18 September they had destroyed over 400 enemy aircraft and gliders. Ten days later the 5th Army, now able to leave the beaches, made rapid inroads and captured all the airfields in the Foggia area. This enabled the air corps to carry out all necessary repairs and servicing to their aircraft and enjoy a brief rest before the affray started again.

The tide had started to turn and after the announcement that the Italian military forces had surrendered, almost 250 Italian pilots flew their aircraft to Sicily to join the Allies. It wasn't until 13 October 1943, when Italy formally declared war on Germany, that they were put into action against the Germans. Within days of that happening they were flying top cover for the 82nd Fighter group during attacks on shipping in the Levkas Channel. Not all the Italian sided with the Allies, and those pilots who stayed committed to the German cause, were absorbed into a *Luftwaffe* Geschwader, JG77, as No. 1 Italian Fighter Group. This of course created the possibility that Italian would fight Italian flying identical aircraft in air combat. There is no official record of this happening, but this is not to say that it didn't.

By the beginning of November the Italian airfields were under the control of the Allies. The US 15th Air Force was formed under the command of General Doolittle and was based in the Foggia district. Every Lightning squadron and group in the theatre was assigned to the US 15th Air Force along with the 5th Photo-reconnaissance Group. On the face of it the Germans appeared to be in full retreat, but when they got to Cassino, 90 miles south of Rome, they dug their heels in and mounted an almost unassailable position, that they would hold throughout the winter. At the end of January 1944 British and American troops landed on the beaches at Anzio and that is where they stayed throughout the winter, pinned down by the Germans. The war was not over by any means, the two sides were having to fight for every inch of ground.

The arrival in March 1944 of the latest P-38 Lightnings, the P-38J, allowed the fighters to penetrate deeper into Europe from Italy. Powered by two 1,600 hp V-1710-89/91 engines giving a maximum speed of 420 mph at 25,000 feet and, with larger fuel tanks, a range of 2,300 miles. It was also the first Lightning type to have an adequately heated cockpit which proved to be, a positive boon in the harsh winter environment in which they were

Lieutenant-General Jimmy Doolittle Commander of the US 8th Air Force, about to take-off in a P-38H-5 on a familiarization flight.

operating. One model of the P-38J was fitted with skis but tests were not satisfactory and any thoughts about equipping a large number of the aircraft with this type of undercarriage were dismissed.

The P-38J was listed as having a basic weight of 13,700 pounds, a combat weight of 17,500 pounds and a maximum weight of 22,000 pounds. The maximum bombload for the P-38J was officially given as 4,000 pounds, but there were numerous accounts of the aircraft carrying a load of 5,200 pounds. This was made up by carrying two 2,000 pound bombs between the engine nacelles and the fuselage, and four 300 pound bombs outboard of the engines. This made the P-38 Lightning the highest bomb load carrying single-seat fighter of World War Two.

The heated cockpit in the P-38J included a hot air defroster which the pilot could direct along any part of the canopy, enabling him to maintain visibility under icy conditions. Another innovation was provided within the electrical circuitry with the installation of circuit beakers in place of fuses. The P-38J as also the first to be fitted with a rocket-launch system. Rockets had been tested on the G-model back in the United States and so successful were they, that kits were rushed to the European Theatre for installation on the P-38Js. They consisted of two pods each with three tubes mounted close to the fuselage. They fired a 4.5-inch spin-stabilised rocket from each of the tubes. The enthusiasm for the rockets was quickly dampened when it was discovered that when operated under battle conditions, the rocket launchers caused severe airflow problems and the firing circuits proved to be unreliable.

Modifications were made resulting in a zero-length system which consisted of ten 5-inch fin-stabilised rockets, five under each wing, in a step-down

P-38J of the 370th Fighter Group, 401st Fighter Squadron, 9th Air Force on the former German nightfighter base at Florennes, Belgium. (Me 410 remains in the foreground)

cluster earning the design the name of the *Christmas Tree Launcher*. This was the only truly successful rocket launcher fitted to the P-38 Lightning.

The new J-model was put to the test on 2 April 1944 when the 82nd Fighter Group were called in to carry out the initial escort for one of the largest bombing raids of the war, the raids on the aircraft factories and ball-bearing factories at Steyr, Austria by the Fifteenth Air Force. On their way to the target the force was jumped by over 50 Me 109s, Fw 190s and Macchi 202s who met the force head-on. It was obvious that the intention was to draw the P-38 Lightnings away from the bomber force and allow another formation of fighters which had been stalking the force from 35,000 feet. But the Lightnings would not be drawn away and managed to shoot down three of the Me 109s on the first pass. Twenty minutes later the Allied formation was joined by North American P-47 Thunderbolts from the 325th Fighter Group who immediately got stuck into the German fighters. One hour later as the force arrived over the target area, the escort was relieved of its duty by the arrival of P-38 Lightnings of the 1st Fighter Group. Within minutes they were involved in repelling an attack by 70 enemy fighters, but when the P-38 Lightnings of the 14th Fighter Group arrived there were in excess of 80 Lightnings and only four enemy fighters got through to the bombers. Two of those were shot down and the remaining two headed for home badly damaged.

As the first wave of bombers left the target area after dropping their deadly cargoes, a swarm of some 50 Me 110s and 210s, escorted by ten Me

The P-38L-1 taxiing out for trials armed with fourteen rockets mounted beneath the wings. This gave the aircraft a firepower that was equal to a Navy cruiser's six-inch broadside – a formidable piece of kit.

109s, raced in firing rockets. They were intercepted by the escort fighters from the 48th Fighter Squadron, who accounted for twelve of the aircraft in a matter of just 20 minutes. The 37th Fighter Squadron, who had been flying top cover during the raid, intercepted another formation of German fighters moving in to attack and shot down eight of them. The enemy fighters withdrew as the bombers left the area, which enabled the remaining American fighters to regroup and escort their charges to safety. The P-38 Lightnings suffered no losses and the pilots expressed their sheer delight

P-38 Lightning with modified drop-tanks for carrying wounded personnel. The idea was not adopted.

F-4C of 90th Photographic Reconnaissance Wing in Italy.

with the new P-38J model after its baptism of fire. One pilot, Lieutenant Robert Siedman, was particularly delighted as he accounted for three Me 109s and declared that if Hitler had realised that `this little Jewish boy had dispatched three of his aircraft, he would go mad.'

Such was the fear that the P-38 Lightnings had instilled into the *Luftwaffe's* fighter pilots that it caused one of them, *Leutnant* Peter Henn, to write in his book, `*The Last Battle*',

> `Let him be pursued by Lightnings, Let his aircraft ring under the bursts like a coat of mail beneath sword thrusts or half blind with blood, let him be forced to extricate himself from the cockpit and sway down in the void, the sky, the earth, the sky, the earth, Mein Gott let this soon be over.'

P-38Js of the 370th Fighter Group, 401st Fighter Squadron, 7th Air Force ETO (European Theatre of Operations), equipped with 500-lb. bombs, about to take off to attack von Rundstedt's troops during the Battle of the Bulge through the Ardennes – Winter 1944.

The raids continued unabated, and as the German *Luftwaffe's* aircraft presence diminished the Allied aircraft grew from strength to strength. By the end of May 1944 the 15th Air Force was capable of sending escorts consisting of 200 P-38 Lightnings, 50 North American P-47 Thunderbolts and P-51 Mustangs. They attacked the railroads to such an extent that almost all rail traffic in Italy was at a standstill. On 4 June Allied troops entered Rome and seized control of Italy. There were token pockets of

F-5E of the 90th Photographic Reconnaissance Wing in Italy.

F-5A on its landing approach and about to touch down in Italy.

resistance but these were quickly dealt with and the push into Germany and Austria suddenly became a reality. The Allied invasion on D-Day 6 June, shifted the focus of war to France. The Allied offensive continued relentlessly in France, whilst the German defensive position in the Northern Apennines was holding and preventing the Allies from breaking out of Italy. Despite all the progress the Allies realised that the war was far from over.

One of the Axis powers that was an unknown quantity to the Allies was Hungary. At the beginning of the war Hungary had allied itself with Nazi

P-38 Lightnings of the 8th Air Force closing in on a bomber formation took take up their positions as escorts for the mission.

Germany to fight against the Soviet Union and was supplied with aircraft by the *Luftwaffe*. It is an accepted fact their the Hungarians wanted no confrontation with the Western Allies and had made no secret that their fight was against the Soviet Union. One of the groups of the *Magyar Királyi Honvéd Légierö* (Royal Hungarian Air Force) that fought against the Soviet Union was 5/1 Group commanded by Major Aladár Heppes. He already had accounted for four Soviet aircraft and was ordered to organise a new group, the 101st Fighter Group. This had been formed to combat the heavy raids that were taking place on the oil refineries outside Budapest and the nitrogen works at Pét. At the onset of the war the Hungarians had hoped that their forces would be concentrated against the Soviet Union and that contact with the Western Allied forces would be minimal, but as time went on the large bomber raids that were to follow put an end to this. Attacking Soviet bomber formations that were escorted by the Soviet's rapidly dwindling fighter force with three or four fighters, was one thing, but fighting formations of 600 plus heavily armed Allied bombers and their heavily armed escorts was something completely different.

One of the first major encounters was on 14 June 1944 when Boeing B-17Gs and North American B-24H bombers from the 55th Bombardment Wing, escorted by Lockheed P-38J Lightnings from the 14th Fighter Group,

Photograph taken from a B-17 bomber as P-38 Lightnings of the 38th Fighter Squadron, 8th Air Force fly cover for B-17 bombers on a mission over Germany.

were on a mission to attack the oil refineries just outside Budapest and the nitrogen works at Pét. Earlier Lightnings of the 95th Fighter Squadron, supported by Lightnings from the 82nd Fighter Group's 96th and 97th Fighter Squadrons, had attacked the Hungarian airfield at Kecskemét. Whilst the 95th carried out a surprise low-level attack on the Me 323 *Gigant* transporters belonging to *Transportgeschwader 5* (Transport Wing 5) on the ground, the remaining two squadrons flew the perimeter drawing the fire from the anti-aircraft guns. As the Lightnings raced across the airfield destroying five of the Me 323s, they were followed by Lightnings from the other two squadrons who bombed the airfield's two hangars, destroying both of them.

While the bombers from the 55th Bombardment Wing approached the oil refineries they were intercepted by 32 Me 109G-6s of the Hungarian 101st Fighter Group and 80 Me 109s and Focke-Wulf Fw 190s of the 8th *Jagddivision*. The rear of the Wing was escorted by P-38J Lightnings of the 37th, 48th and 49th Fighter Squadrons from the 14th Fighter Group, a total of 48 fighter aircraft. The bombers went to their targets in waves and dispatched their deadly cargoes with devastating accuracy, confirmed by a

F-5A photo-reconnaissance Lightning on a mission over Germany.

column of smoke from the refinery that rose to 25,000 feet. The cover plan for the fighters was that as the bombers went in, the three escorting fighter squadrons would skirt around the bombing area and meet the bombers as they came out of the bombing zone. As the fighter pilots made their way around the zone they had a birds-eye view of the attack and to their cost spent more time looking at the raid than around them. Suddenly excited voices clamoured over the radios describing the raid when one of the voices cried '51s high at 10 o'clock'. Seconds later another voice broke in '51s hell, those are 109s.' The next minute all hell broke loose as 32 Me 109s and 28 Focke-Wulf Fw 190s dived in to attack the 49th Fighter Squadron. The

P-38 Lightning escorting 8th Air Force bombers over Germany await German interceptors.

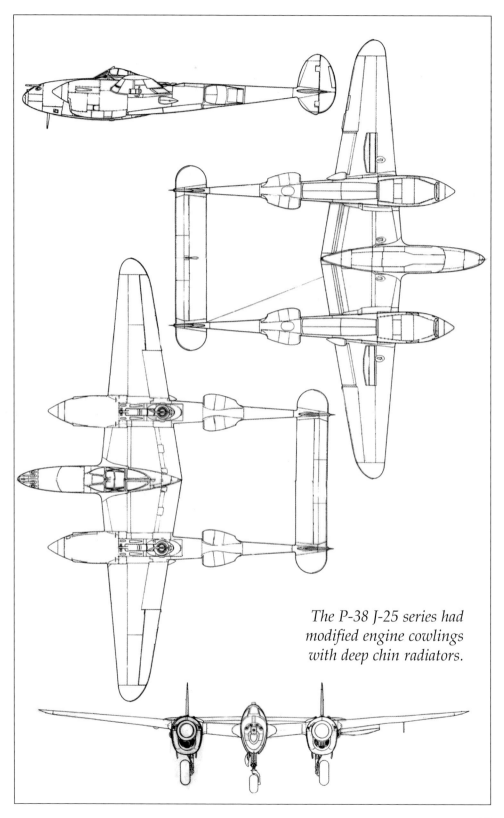

The P-38 J-25 series had modified engine cowlings with deep chin radiators.

ensuing mêlée resulted in the destruction of thirteen Me 109s and eight Fw 190s with the loss of five P-38 Lightnings. A large number of aircraft on both sides were badly damaged but two lessons were learnt that day;

1. Stop rubbernecking when on a raid and watch the sky around you.
2. Don't underestimate the opposition especially when they are flying P-38 Lightnings or *Létrák* (Stepladders) as the Hungarians called them.

Meanwhile in the Far East, the legendary aviator Charles Lindbergh was visiting various squadrons. During the visit he showed the P-38 pilots a technique which, with proper engine settings and fuel management, would increase the range of the aircraft and allow it to stay aloft for almost 12 hours. It was a technique that had been long known to veteran mail carrying pilots, but one that had not been taught at flying school. On 28 July 1944 he was invited to fly with the squadron on a reconnaissance mission, flying the deputy Group Commander, Lieutenant-Colonel Meryl Smith's, P-38 Lightning. During the mission the squadron came across a number of Japanese transports with escorts and, in the ensuing mêlée, Lindbergh shot down a Mitsubishi Ki-51 (Sonia). The incident was not declared until after the war because of the possible repercussions for allowing a 'civilian' to take

P-38 Lightning shepherding a Boeing B-17 to its target over Germany.

an active part in a combat raid.

A second invasion started on 15 August in Southern France supported by P-38 Lightnings from the 1st and 14th Fighter Groups based in Corsica. In the first five days the two groups had flown over 1,000 sorties with the loss of 23 Lightnings. Bombers from Foggia were escorted by P-38 Lightnings from the 82nd Fighter Group and pounded the enemy positions. Meanwhile in Italy the lack of opposition from the *Luftwaffe* prompted the

P-38J-5, 384th FS, 364th FG, US 8th AF.
Honington, UK, April 1944.

P-38J-5-LO, 79th FS, 20th FG, US 8th AF. UK, 1943.
(Right) marking on inside of both tail fins.

P-38J, 428th FS, 474th FG, US 9th AF.

P-38J, 430th FS, 474th FG, US 9th AF.

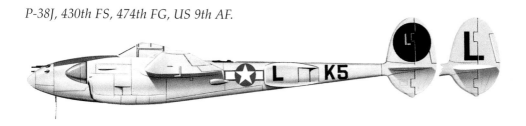

P-38J-15-LO, 43-28550, 55th FS, 20th FG, US 8th AF. UK, 1944.

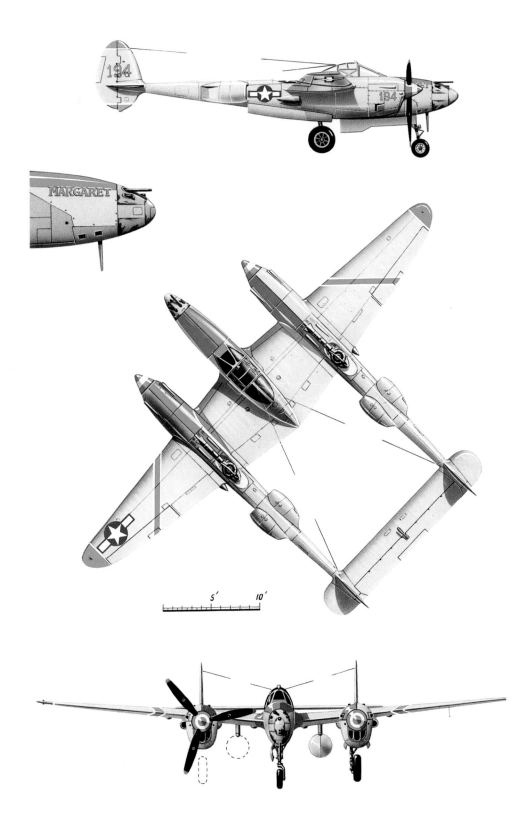

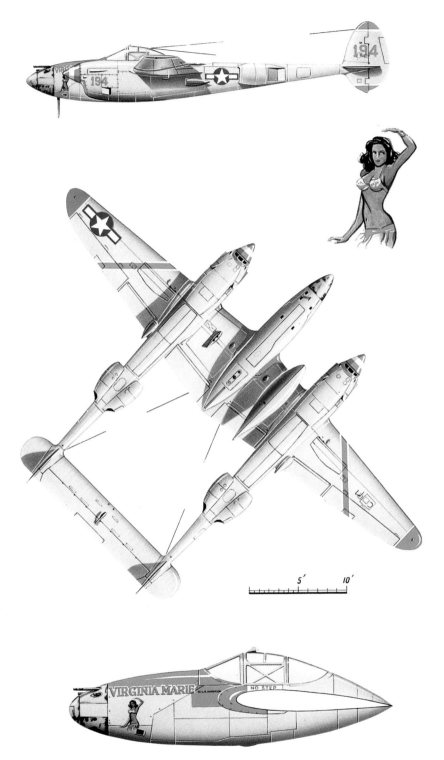

P-38J, 433rd FS, 475th FG, US 5th AF, Dutch New Guinea, 1943/44.
'Virginia Marie' flown by Lt C Robert Anderson.

P-38J, 18th FG, US 12th AF, Philippines, July 1944.

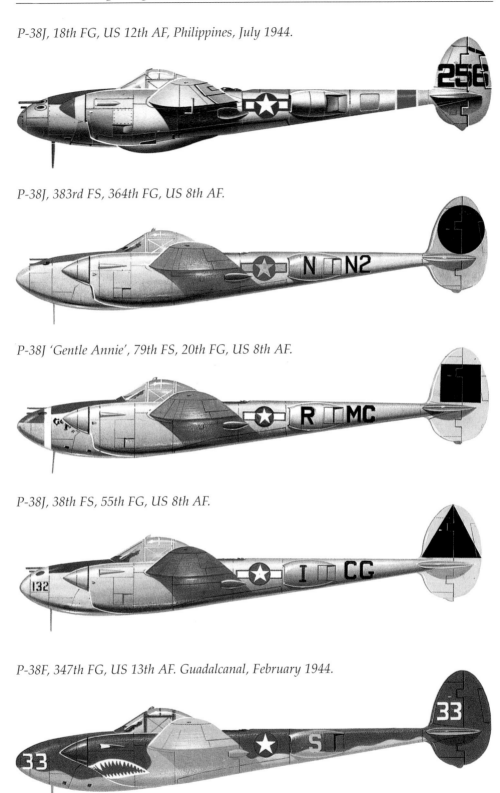

P-38J, 383rd FS, 364th FG, US 8th AF.

P-38J 'Gentle Annie', 79th FS, 20th FG, US 8th AF.

P-38J, 38th FS, 55th FG, US 8th AF.

P-38F, 347th FG, US 13th AF. Guadalcanal, February 1944.

P-38J, 8th FG, US 5th AF. Cape Gloucester, SWPA, 1944.

P-38J, 338th FS, 55th FG, US 8th AF.

P-38J, 433rd FS, 475th FG, US 5th AF. Dutch New Guinea, 1944.
Flown by Major Warren E Lewis, OC.

P-38J, 433rd FS, 475th FG, US 5th AF. Philippines, 1944.

P-38J, 18th FG, US 5th AF. Philippines.

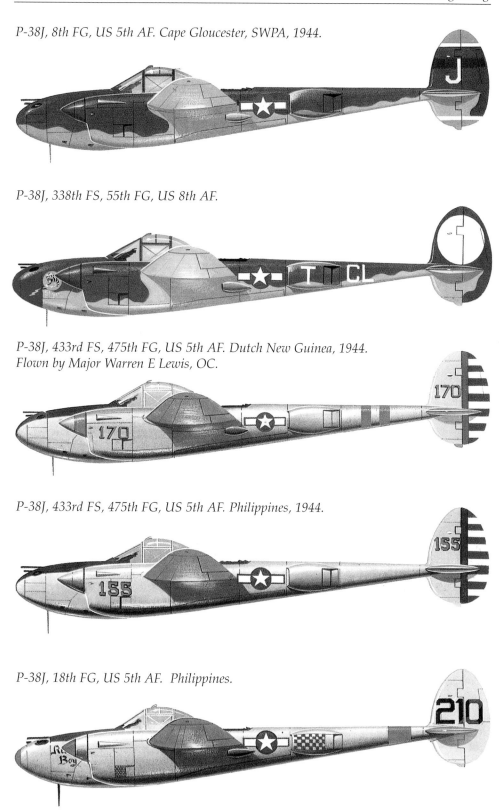

F-4C, 8th Photographic Reconnaissance Group. India.

P-38J, 433rd FS, 475th FG, US 5th AF, Dutch New Guinea, 1943/44.

P-38J, 338th FS, 55th FG, US 8th AF. ETO

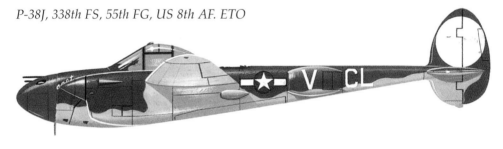

P-38H, 343rd FS, 55th FG, US 8th AF. ETO.

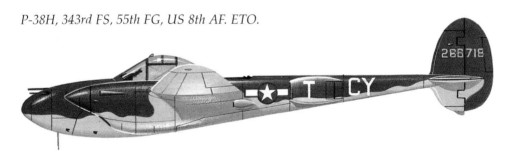

P-38J, 401st FS, 370th FG, US 9th AF. ETO.

P-38J, 485th FS, 370th FG, US 9th AF. ETO.

P-38J, 474th FS, 429th FG, US 9th AF. ETO.

P-38J 'Pathfinder', probably of the 107th TRC, 67th TRG, US 9th AF. ETO.

F-5A, GR 2/33, Free French Air Force, La Marsa, Tunisia, 1943.

F-5B, GR 2/33, Free French Air Force, Bastia, Corsica, 1944.

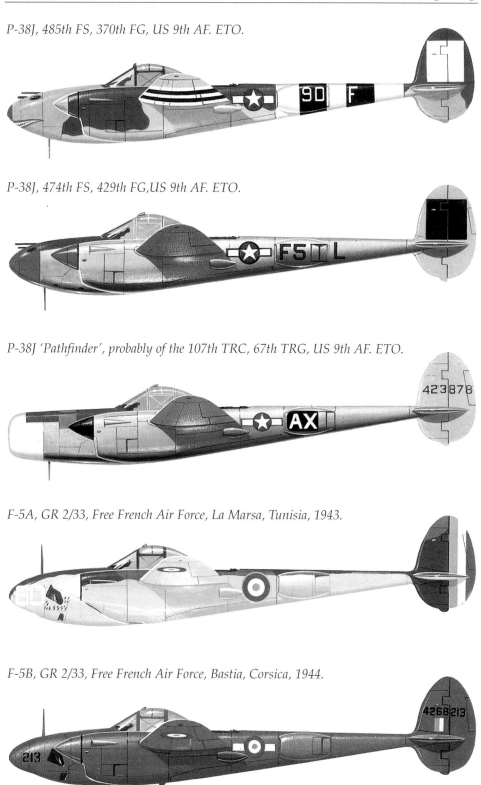

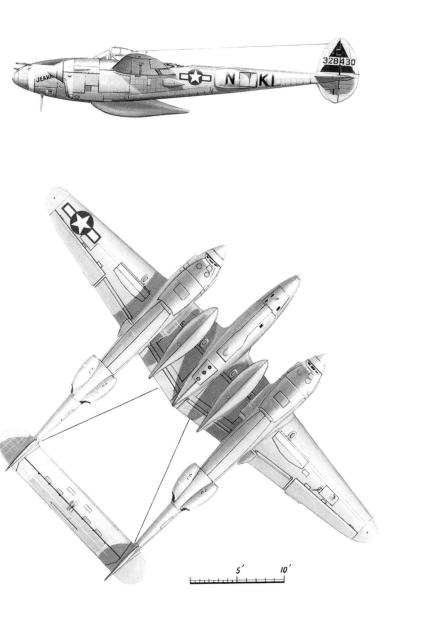

5′   10′

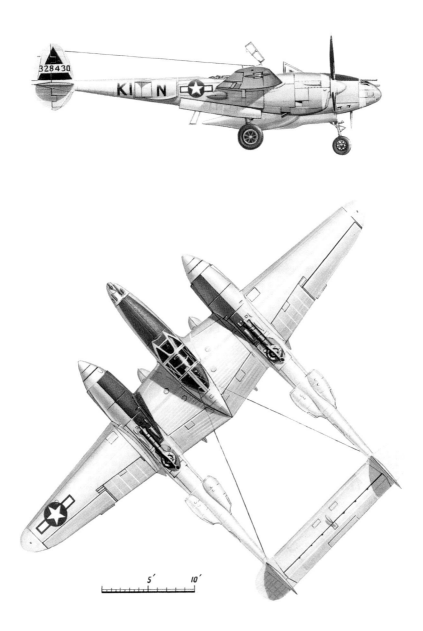

P-38J-25 Series had modified engine cowlings with deep 'chin' radiators.

P-38L, 4th Aerobrigata, Italian Air Force, 1945-6.

F-5F, 3rd Aerobrigata RT, Italian Air Force, 1945-6.

P-38L, 4th Aerobrigata, Italian Air Force, 1946.

F-5E, Chinese Nationalist Air Force.

F-5G, Chinese Nationalist Air Force.

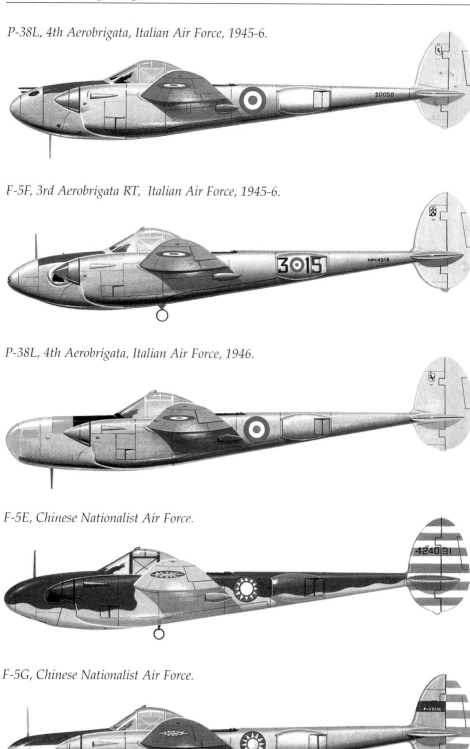

P-38L, Honduras Air Force.

P-38J, 8th FG, Port Moresby, New Guinea, November 1943.

F-5E-2, 43-28329, 34th Photo-Recon. Sqdn., Rennes, France, August 1944.

P-38L, MM4206, 3rd Aerobrigata, Italian Air Force, 1946.

L-322-61 Lightning Mk I, AF106, Special Duties Flight,
Boscombe Down, Summer 1942.

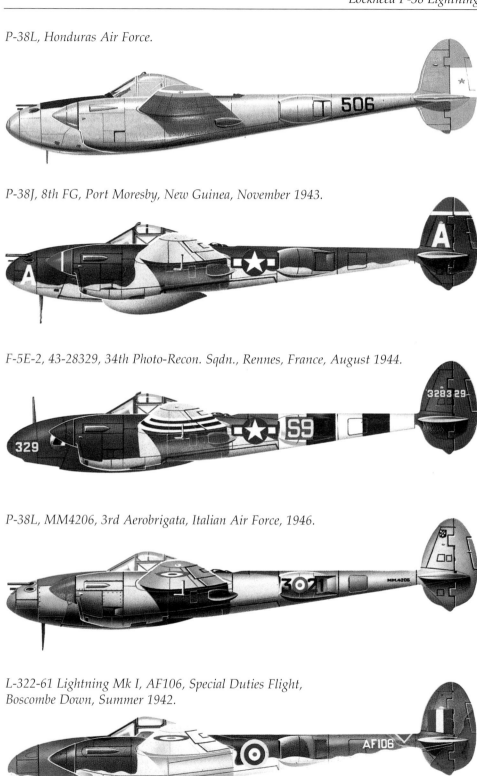

P-38F-1, 14th FG, US 12th AF, Youks-les-Bains, Algeria, December 1942.

P-38J, 430th FS, 474th FG, US 9th AF, Langensalza, May 1945.

P-38M, 44-26865, 'Night Lightning'. Converted from P-38L-5-LO.

P-38J-20-LO, 44-23296, 'Yippee'.
The 5,000th P-38 built.

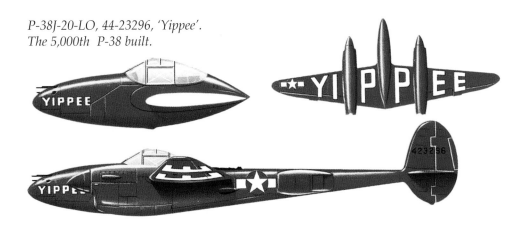

air corps to move the squadrons closer to Germany. In one bizarre incident P-38 Lightnings were escorting a formation of B-24 Mitchells on a bombing raid to Munich, when, as they approached the target, a P-51B Mustang appeared from nowhere and joined the escorts from the 95th Fighter Squadron. As the bombers went into bomb, the fighter escorts carried out strafing runs. With the raid over the formation formed up again with the escorts and headed for home. Suddenly the P-51B Mustang re-appeared and began to make passes in front of the Lightnings. One of the P-38 Lightnings, flown by Lieutenant Hawthorn, had been hit during one of his strafing runs and was running on one engine. The P-51B made a bee-line for him with all its guns blazing, but fortunately Lieutenant Eldon Coulson had been watching the P-51B, concerned with its behaviour, and poured his remaining ammunition into it. The Mustang rolled onto its back and spun into the ground.

It was discovered later that the Germans had flown two captured P-51B Mustangs on a number of occasions, catching Allied aircraft unawares. This of course highlighted the fact that the *Luftwaffe* were running out of aircraft and ideas.

Photograph taken from the waist-gunners position in a Boeing B-17 showing P-38 Lightnings from 94th Squadron, 1st Fighter Group escorting the bombers home.

The 3rd and 5th photo-reconnaissance units were now flying non-stop missions over Germany in their P-38 (F-5)s and were being escorted by P-38J Lightnings from the 82nd Fighter Group. Then at the end of November, the group received the first of the `Droop Snoot' Lightnings. This was a standard P-38J Lightning that had all its nose armament removed and a modified B-17 Flying Fortress nose mounted in its place. The modified P-38J led a squadron of P-38s – renamed B-38s for the missions – and carried out sightings through a Norden bombsight for high-level bombing missions. In the nose of the modified P-38J, a bombardier lay prone, and on a given signal from him, the following B-38s dropped their load of bombs on the selected target. There were risks involved in these operations, inasmuch as the bombardier could not wear a parachute in the very restricted nose section and could not exit the aircraft whilst it was in flight.

P-38 Lightnings from the 1st Fighter Group crossing overhead as they escort the 2nd Bomber Group into Germany.

At the beginning of 1945, in an effort to breach the German defences in the Northern Apennines strafing and bombing missions were carried out around the Arno River area. The 14th Fighter Group accounted for more than 100 trains, severely damaging the German supply lines. In March the breakthrough started and the 5th Army breached the German defences supported by P-38 Lightnings. It was also around this time that the Allies came into contact with the Messerschmitt Me 262, the worlds first operational jet fighter. It happened when four Lightnings from the 49th Fighter Squadron, escorting an F-4 on a photo-reconnaissance mission over Munich, were `bounced' by a German jet. Surprised, to say the least, the Lightnings managed to elude the Me 262 but were unable to get a shot off at him. One can only imagine the tales told by the pilots when they

A formation of P-38 Lightnings of the 1st Fighter Group returning to their base after escorting B-24 bombers to their targets over Austria.

P-38 of the 9th Air Force.

returned. Fortunately for the Allies it was an aircraft that had arrived far too late to have any impact upon the war.

Almost at the same time as the 5th Army made the break through from Italy, the Fifteenth Air Force, escorted by Lightnings from the 1st Air Group, carried out a major bombing raid on the heart of Germany – Berlin. The

Boeing B-17G Flying Fortresses repaying the favour as they escort a damaged P-38 Lightning with one of its engines feathered after being hit by flak, back to its base in England.

Luftwaffe could offer little or no resistance to the Allied aircraft and anti-aircraft fire from the ground was almost non-existent. Allied aircraft roamed at will and carried out low-level strafing attacks against the weakened defences and the retreating German forces.

German resistance in the Apennine Mountains however was still fierce, so the 1st Air Group assigned a number of P-38 Lightning squadrons to the area to soften up the German defences. In one raid on 11 April 1944 over 40 P-38 Lightnings attacked the railway facilities and destroyed 84 railway engines and 50 oil trucks, but it cost them fifteen aircraft. By the end of April almost all the railway lines and bridges supplying the German defences had been severed, so when the Allied advance swept through German resistance was broken. Trapped between the British 8th Army and the American 5th Army it was only a matter of days before over a million Germans had surrendered and the war in Italy was over. The Lightning squadrons re-grouped and were assigned to the European Theatre of Operations.

CHAPTER FIVE

'...if they were not there, then they were German.'

In England in 1944 preparations were under way for the invasion of mainland Europe. Lockheed P-38 Lightnings, de Havilland Mosquitos and North American Mustangs were making photo-reconnaissance flights over the France and Belgium. No particular place was overflown more than the others in an effort not to raise suspicions as to where the landings were to take place. The German defence lines were photographed from Holland to the borders of Spain. Photographs were taken from high, medium and low altitudes and occasionally a very low level, high speed run along the beaches, was carried out by Lightnings. The runs were carried out along the beaches at Normandy and the Pas de Calais so as not to draw attention to the invasion spot. The aircraft were fitted with sideways-looking and forward-looking oblique cameras in order to give close-up shots of the more important objectives. The reason behind this was to try and give the coxswains of the landing craft a view of what to expect when they headed their craft for the shore.

Sorties were flown against all the 92 German radar stations that were sited along the French coast. All but sixteen of these stations were put out of action just before D-Day and not one of those that was still operational overlooked the invasion area. But these radar sites were taken out at a high cost to the Allied air forces as they were extremely well defended. Plans for the D-Day landings were formulated and one of the major thoughts behind the planning was how to convince the Germans that the landings were going to take place in the Pas de Calais area and not Normandy. It was also decided to attack the railway system in a way that would isolate Normandy and prevent any reinforcements being rushed to the area once the Germans had realised where the attack was taking place. It was hoped that the Germans would think that the attack was going to happen in Calais and Le Havre areas and rush defenders there. Seventy-two major railway objectives were chosen, 39 in the western section of Germany and 33 in

France and Belgium. These would include rolling stock, marshalling yards, repair shops, railway junctions, bridges and long stretches of track. The aircraft selected for these strafing and bombing missions were P-38 Lightnings and de Havilland Mosquitos. Whilst the attacks were going on, the US 9th Air Force was to attack airfields and bridges over the River Seine. The idea was that the moment the invasion began the Germans would rush reinforcements to the area, and if access was denied or severely restricted to them then Allied forces would be able to gain a major foothold on the mainland.

On the eve of 6 June 1944 the Allied air forces had achieved aerial superiority over the *Luftwaffe* which prompted General Eisenhower, to say, in his pre-invasion address to the combined troops, 'Don't worry about the

F-5 (P-38) photo-reconnaissance Lightning catching, unaware, German soldiers on parade.

P-38 Lightnings with D-Day markings sweeping across the channel to attack the retreating German army.

planes overhead...they will be ours.'

P-38 Lightnings in their invasion livery of black and white stripes on the wings and fuselage, were among 3,700 Allied fighters, fighter/bombers and bombers preparing to fly across the channel and wreak havoc amongst the *Luftwaffe* and German Army. As darkness crept over the south coast of England a huge armada of ships silently slid out of ports along the coast, while night fighters maintained non-stop patrols over the English Channel. As dawn broke, the air along the coast of southern England was filled with the roar of thousands of aircraft engines as they prepared to support the landings. High above Calais and Le Havre, bombers dropped bundles of aluminium foil which spread like clouds and confused the enemy radar operators into thinking that an aerial armada was on its way. Even dummy paratroopers were dropped behind the enemy batteries in these areas in an attempt to confuse them even more.

As the invasion armada crossed the English Channel, twenty RAF anti-submarine aircraft, combed the water off the Western Approaches for U-boats. The Sunderland flying boats of Coastal Command were scouring the surface of the sea between the coast of southern Ireland and Brittany. This was an enormous task because of the vast open sea and the area to be covered. However, it was crucial to the success of the invasion, as any U-boat heading up the channel would have to run on the surface because the distance was too far to run submerged and had it spotted the invasion fleet could have warned their High Command. Such was the intensity that had any U-boat commander seen the high profile searches going on he would have kept well out of the way.

Lancaster and Halifax bombers from the RAF and the B-17 Flying

The first P-38 Lightning to land on an American airfield in France after the D-Day landings.

Fortresses and B-24 Liberators from the USAAF carpet bombed the batteries along the Normandy coast led by Mosquitos of the Pathfinder squadrons. P-38 Lightnings attacked the radar stations, still operational, as well as that were the surrounding fortifications, in preparation for the largest airborne assault operation, that consisted of three divisions and their equipment. In the early hours of the morning of 6 June, 104 Horsa and Waco gliders carrying the US Airborne, struggled into the air packed with troops and equipment and headed across the channel. At the same time 98 Horsa and Hamilcars carrying a British airborne division and their equipment were hauled into the air behind a variety of Dakotas, Stirlings and Halifaxes.

Throughout the night six groups of P-38 Lightnings from the US 8th and

P-38s of the 55th Fighter Group, 38th Fighter Squadron taxing out for take-off at Warningford, Northant, UK.

9th Air Forces had flown on a rota basis over the invasion fleet as it crossed the channel. The P-38 was chosen for this role because of its distinctive twin boom shape which was unlikely to be confused by the naval gunners on the ships with anything the *Luftwaffe* had in the air at the time.

As the invasion force approached the coast two RAF Douglas Bostons of No. 324 (French) Squadron, raced along the shoreline laying a smoke screen, while P-38 Lightnings hammered the coastal defences with cannon fire. Every ten minutes Bostons replaced the smoke screen and wave after wave of P-38s continued their relentless battering of the German defences. British warships laying off the coast opened up their guns in deafening salvoes, their shells pulverizing the coast line. One pilot remembers watching the battleship HMS *Warspite* open fire with her 15-inch guns in four gun salvoes, in an exchange of gunfire with six 155-mm guns from a shore battery near Trouville. He only realised that he was too close when one of the one-ton shells whizzed in front of his aircraft. His was one of the fighter

The P-38 `Pathfinder' showing the extended nose that housed the ground-mapping radar that enabled the aircraft to lead other bomb-laden P-38 Lightnings to targets that were covered in cloud.

aircraft that were flying as spotters for the gun-crews of the battleships and cruisers that lay off-shore.

The news of the landings were a total surprise to the *Luftwaffe* as no German reconnaissance aircraft had picked up any activity and the strength of the invasion fleet shocked them. What was even more disturbing was that the German High Command had been told by *Feldmarschall* Erwin Rommel that if there was an invasion the Normandy beaches was the most likely place where the Allies would land. But Hitler's military advisors were convinced that it would be the Pas de Calais region because that was the narrowest point between England and mainland Europe. Some of the *Luftwaffe* fighters and fighter/bombers managed to get in the air and approach the beaches, but the aerial cover by the British and American fighters prevented them getting through. Two Focke-Wulf Fw 190s of *Jagdgeschwader 26* flown by *Oberst* Josef Priller, the *Jagdgeschwader's* commanding officer, and *Unteroffizier* Heinz Wodarczyk managed to carry out a low-level strafing attack on Sword Beach but were chased away by defending fighters as they started to make a second run.

Flak damage to the wings and tail of a P-38 Lightning of the 79th Fighter Squadron, 20th Fighter Group.

F-5 of the French Air Force preparing to taxi.

F-5E of the French Air Force.

As the first wave of troops established their positions on the beaches, *Luftwaffe* bases throughout France, Belgium and Germany were put on red alert. Fifty Focke-Wulf Fw 190s of III/*Schlachtgeschwader 4* were ordered from their bases in southern and eastern France to bases at Laval and Tours. The practice, during deployments such as these, was to carry a mechanic tucked into the rear of the fuselage so that the aircraft could be maintained when it arrived at its new base. Obviously there was no room for a parachute for the mechanic: even if there was it would have been extremely difficult, if not impossible, to get out in the case of an emergency. As the Fw 190s approached the area, they were attacked by P-51 Mustangs, P-47 Thunderbolts and P-38 Lightnings. Five of the Fw 190s were shot down in the first encounter, the pilots refused to bail out because of their mechanics and all ten men in the aircraft were killed. A number of the other Fw 190s were severely damaged with the result that in the late afternoon of the same day, only thirteen were able to carry out any kind of sortie. The thirteen aircraft were split into three raiding forces; the first was dealt with by defending aircraft, but the remaining two managed to get through only to be met by withering anti-aircraft fire from the beaches. Twenty Junkers Ju 88 bombers attempted to bomb the beachheads but were intercepted. Nine were shot down and the remainder were forced to discharge their bomb loads harmlessly into the sea in order to escape.

With the Allied troops now streaming inland from the Normandy beaches, temporary airstrips were being set up and the first of the P-38 Lightnings of the 367th Fighter Group, 9th Air Force, touched down just days after the landings. From their base they attacked the retreating German Army and in one mission they attacked *Luftwaffe* airfields at Clastres, Peronne and Rosieries where, despite intense anti-aircraft fire, they caused severe damage to the aircraft and facilities there. They also encountered stiff opposition in the air and accounted for a number of enemy fighters. Despite being short of fuel the group attacked a supply train and a road convoy on their way home. They received a Distinguished Unit Citation for the raid.

The mass retreat of the German Army produced lucrative targets for the Allied air forces. This was never more apparent than on 13 August 1944, when a lone P-47 Thunderbolt from the 366th Fighter Group on an armed reconnaissance flight spotted what looked like trees in the road. On closer inspection he saw that they were camouflaged tanks and, called up for support to be joined by other P-47 Thunderbolts from the 366th and P-38

F-5P of the French Air Force at Bordeaux.

lightnings from the 367th Fighter Group. When the aircraft raced into strafe the tanks with cannon fire they realised that they had come across around 30 heavily camouflaged fuel tankers that were refuelling around a dozen tanks. When they left the scene there was a line of flaming vehicles more than a mile long and, what is more, they had blocked the road to prevent more German troops leaving. On their way back they encountered a huge convoy of some 200 vehicles and exhausted their ammunition on these, leaving a trail of destruction behind them.

A second Allied assault on the French Mediterranean coast on 15 August was also carried out with the benefit of surprise. There were *Luftwaffe* units in the area, but they consisted of Junkers Ju 88 and Dornier Do 217 bombers, with no fighters. A single *Gruppe* from Italy was rushed to the area, but the landing force was well protected by aircraft from aircraft carriers and was quickly disposed of. *Luftwaffe* units in France were being decimated by the ferocity and surprise of the attacks and to help them withdraw and re-group, four *Gruppen* were transferred from Germany to cover the withdrawal. One of these was *II/Jagdgeschwader 6* who flew to Herpy near Rheims. Their airfield consisted of a cow pasture and their hangars were openings in the trees that surrounded the pasture. It was a well sited airfield, inasmuch as whilst they were not flying, all the aircraft and tented accommodation were in amongst the trees, a herd of cows was then driven into the field to graze. The cows gave a countryside feel to the area and also wiped out any tracks in the field that may have been left behind by the aircraft.

During one raid carried out by the *Gruppe,* they surprised twelve P-38 Lightnings of 367th Fighter Group in the act of strafing the airfield at Clastres and shot down six of them. The assistance call brought two squadrons of the P-38 Lightnings into the fight who quickly turned the fight around and accounted for sixteen Focke-Wulf Fw 190s shot down and more than a dozen badly damaged. The *Luftwaffe* could not afford losses on this scale, it was not so much the aircraft, but the loss of the pilots that was becoming the major cause for concern. A large number of their pilots were inexperienced in dogfighting and becoming easy meat to the more experienced Allied pilots.

The withdrawal from France gained momentum as more and more Allied troops and equipment came ashore. One despairing retreating German soldier put it succinctly when he said;

> *'If the aircraft were camouflaged they were British. If they were silver they were American and if they were not there, then they were German.'*

The air war over France was, in effect, over.

CHAPTER SIX

'...you can't turn back because of frostbite.'

The affection for the P-38 Lightning shown by pilots in the Pacific and the Mediterranean Theatres of the war, was not shared by their compatriots in Europe. This was because of shortcomings they discovered in the P-38 Lightning that did not measurably affect their fellow pilots in the other Theatres of the war. One of these, which was a very important factor, was the lack of windscreen defrosting and cockpit heating. Although on the face of it not one of the most serious of shortcomings in warmer climates, when pilots were flying over Europe in the winter months they were often forced to fly at heights exceeding 30,000 feet, something their colleagues in the other Theatres did not often experience. The extreme cold experienced by pilots at these heights affected their judgement and aggressiveness, and restricted the length of time they could stay in the air. Pilots would wear layer after layer of clothing and look like huge bears as they waddled to their aircraft. Cases of severe frostbite to hands and feet were not uncommon amongst the pilots and the term `airborne ice-waggon' was not an endearing epithet for the Lightning. This seriously diminished the P-38 Lightnings capabilities and despite a large number of complaints by both pilots, squadron commanders and group commanders, nothing was done until the arrival of the P-38J model. What angered the pilots was the modifications required to resolve the problem would, on the face of it, not be unsurmountable.

Lockheed test pilot Tony LeVier was ordered to go to Europe to demonstrate the full capabilities of the P-38 Lightning and to persuade the squadron pilots that it was not the freezing unresponsive monster that many of them considered it to be. On arriving he discovered that many of the complaints the pilots had were justified to a certain extent. The problem was that the aircraft had been developed and tested in California and had never been subjected to tests at high altitude in cold weather. As one pilot put it, `If and engine quits on you that is something that can happen, if the turbo-supercharger goes kaput that can happen, but if you have to turn back from a mission because of frostbite that is something that should never have happened.' Inevitably Tony LeVier's report back to Lockheed was one that hastened the fitting of heaters into the cockpits of the next generation of P-38 Lightnings.

The Weiheim marshalling yards in Germany under attack by P-38 Lightnings. Note the P-38 Lightning at lower right.

Tony LeVier toured the United Kingdom visiting all the USAAF bases that had P-38 Lightnings. At each of the bases he carried out tests on random aircraft experiencing some of the poor maintenance problems that the squadron pilots were having to contend with. These problems were not because of a lack of commitment by the mechanics and fitters, but more from the lack of spares. The maintenance crews were having to make – do as best they could under the most difficult of circumstances in an effort to keep the aircraft flying. On a couple of occasions Tony LeVier lost an engine which gave him the opportunity to show the pilots exactly how to deal with this problem if they ever found themselves in a similar position.

P-38H-5s of the 338th Fighter Squadron, 55 Fighter Group preparing for take off from the 91st Bomber Group's base at Bassingbourn, Cambridgeshire, UK.

When he arrived at the USAAF base at Honington, the home of 364th Fighter Group, he found himself in an environment of completely green pilots who had just arrived from training in the United States. Almost none of them had flown an aircraft above 20,000. This which enabled LeVier to conduct a series of lectures that covered the best operating procedures for the P-38 at altitude and the problems of compressibility in high speed flight. Flying the P-38 in training and under a few simulated battle conditions was nothing to what these pilots were going to have to face when they tangled with the battle hardened Messerschmitt Bf 109 and Focke-Wulf Fw 190 pilots of the German *Luftwaffe*. Tony LeVier stressed to them that the P-38 was in a class of its own when at low level, but to tangle with the German fighters at heights of 30-35,000 feet was futile and potentially lethal. At low level the

113

P-38 was capable of making very tight manoeuvres and on a number of occasions when, at very low level, they had an Me 109 on their tail, the P-38 pilot could pull a hard turn to the left which would often cause the Me 109

P-38 Lightnings of the 38th Fighter Squadron, 55th Fighter Group 'beating up' their airfield at Nuthampstead, Hertfordshire, UK, after a successful escort mission.

to stall out and snap-roll into the ground as it tried to follow.

On his return to Lockheed, Tony LeVier approached the design engineers and emphasised the need for dive brakes to be fitted. Satisfied that they had an answer to preventing the P-38 entering the 'Shock Stall', they assembled 425 dive flap kits to be sent to the European Theatre to be fitted on the P-38 Lightnings that were already operational. They were loaded on to a Douglas C-54 four-engined transport for delivery to England but the aircraft never arrived. Rumours were rife on how the aircraft went missing, some say in was shot down in mid-Atlantic by Focke-Wulf Fw 200 Condor, others that it crashed due to engine trouble. One even said that it was shot down by an over-zealous Spitfire pilot as it approached England. Whatever happened it never arrived and by the time Lockheed had got around to replacing the kits they were already being fitted to the latest model, the P-38J Lightning. One wonders if all this would have been necessary if the 'powers that be' had not decided to embark on that disastrous publicity stunt with the prototype XP-38.

There were other problems that the pilots discovered but none of them appeared to be worthy of consideration until the appearance of the P-38J. Bolt-on dive flaps that were deemed to be a necessary modification in April 1943 did not appear until June 1944. Problems with the inter-cooler system in the supercharger was the cause of a number of engine failures when at

The first of the P-38J models at Langford Lodge, Ireland.

high altitude. It wasn't until the appearance of the P-38H model that this was resolved with the fitting of automatic engine controls. Such was the dissatisfaction of the pilots with the P-38 Lightningthat it was often known disparagingly as 'Allison time bombs'.

Nevertheless the P-38 Lightning continued to escort long-range bombers on raids over Germany, now aided by the North American P-51 Mustang which was fitted with auxiliary fuel tanks. One of the biggest raids of the war took place on 29 January 1944 when 900 Boeing B-17 Flying Fortresses of the US 8th Air Force, carried out a raid on Frankfurt. The escort consisted of twelve fighter groups, including the 55th and 20th Fighter Group with their P-38J Lightnings and 354th Fighter Group with their P-51B Mustangs. Indicative of the enemy's lack of airpower, only 80 of their single-engined and 40 twin-engined fighters took to the air in an attempt to defend the skies over the target. Forty-two enemy aircraft were shot down with the loss of nine P-38 Lightnings, two of which were involved in collisions with Me 109s.

In February 1944, five additional fighter groups, the 370th, 474th, 367th, 364th and 479th, were added to the strengths of the 8th and 9th Air Forces. All were equipped with P-38J Lightnings that had the latest modifications, such as windscreen defrosting and cockpit heating and, a new type of control column. The old `half spectacle' wheel was removed and a rams-horn type installed. The modifying of the control column by removing the

P-38 of the 37th Fighter Squadron, 14th Fighter Group after a wheels-up landing. Earlier the pilot, Lt Thomas W Smith had an almost head-on collision with a Bf 109 in which the latter lost a wing and crashed. The P-38, despit losing an engine and a severed tail section as can be seen in the photograph, managed to limp home.

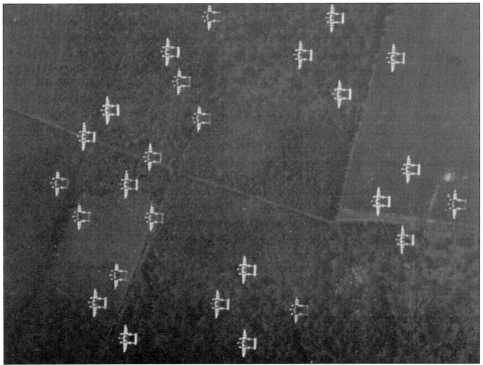

P-38 Lightnings photographed by an F-5 (P-38) photo-reconnaissance Lightning as they made their way across the English countryside toward the Channel.

lower part of the wheel created more leg room for the pilot. Even access to the radio equipment, which up to this point had been a nightmare, was eased by the installation of fast removal Dzus buttons. Large intakes were also installed beneath the propellers and housed core-type radiators, replacing the inter-cooler system that had been contained in the leading edges of the wings. This modification allowed the aircraft to carry an additional 110 gallons of fuel in the wings. These were probably the most combat ready of all the Lightnings that had been built to date.

A change in weather during the week 20 to 25 February 1944, saw the largest raid on Germany take place. One thousand heavy bombers from the 8th and 9th Air Forces and 500 from the 15th Air Force in Italy, pounded German manufacturing plants in Augsburg, Stuttgart and Regensburg. One hundred and eighty P-38 Lightnings from the 20th and 55th Fighter Groups

Close-up of bomb leader's Pathfinder P-38J

together with P-47 Thunderbolts escorted the bombers. Strange as it may seem, whilst the P-38 Lightnings were escorting the bombers, there were no attacks from enemy fighters, but when they were relieved by the P-47 Thunderbolts the Me 109s and Fw 190s swept in.

A number of the Lightning groups received a new modified Lightning – the P-38J-15 or 'Droop Snoot' as it became to be known. This innovation elevated the role of the P-38 Lightning from flying escort to fighter/bomber. Their role of escorting the long-range heavy bombers was still part of their remit, but it had now been strengthened by the North American P-51 Mustang.

The new nose on the P-38s contained ground-mapping radar to enable

The lead fighter bomber 'Droop Snoot' of the 20th FG, US 8th Air Force, Kingscliffe, UK

bomb-aimers to drop 1,000lb bombs through heavy cloud cover. The first of two missions, at the end of April 1944, was carried out by two squadrons from the 55th Fighter Group, each aircraft carrying one drop tank and one 1,000lb bomb. A third squadron flew top cover for them as they approached the target, an airfield at St Dizier. Even with the ground-mapping radar the weather was so atrocious that they had to move to a secondary target, the

Lt Col. James Hall, Commander of the 7th Photo-Reconnaissance Group briefing his pilots at Mount Farm, England prior to the D-Day landings.

airfield at Coulonniers.

The second mission was carried out on the airfield at Gütersloh by 26 P-38J-15s, from two squadrons of the 20th Fighter Group, each aircraft carrying a drop tank and a 1,000-lb bomb. After the bombs had been dropped, all the attacking aircraft then went down low-level and strafed the airfields causing significant damage to both aircraft and personnel. Both raids were extremely successful.

Slowly but surely, in the European Theatre, the P-38 Lightning was being replaced by the P-51 Mustang. Then on Tuesday 6 June 1944 D-Day, or Operation *Overlord* as it was also known, began and P-38 Lightnings were in the thick of the action. All the Allied aircraft taking part were painted with black and white invasion stripes so as to identify them to friendly forces. The P-38s role was to overfly the part of the English Channel that was used to ship the invasion forces to the Normandy beaches. Once the beachheads were secured and the troops began to move inland, the P-38 Lightnings and P-47 Thunderbolts, secure in the knowledge that enemy

P-38 returning from a sortie during the D-Day offensive.

aircraft were no longer a threat to the troops, began strafing attacks on the retreating German forces and the *Luftwaffe's* remaining airfields. There were serious pockets of resistance and a number of Lightnings were shot down, but slowly and surely command of the air swung in favour of the Allies.

As the bombing raids were increased, so the role of escort was given to the P-38 Lightnings as it had been quickly realised that the *Luftwaffe* were extremely reluctant to tangle with them. The Lightnings were accompanied on these missions by the P-47 Thunderbolts as there were in fact 22 P-47 Groups as compared with only seven P-38 Lightning Groups.

As the Lightnings were lost or damaged, they were being replaced by the North American P-51 Mustang, which, with the Merlin-powered engine and auxiliary fuel tanks, was a far better all-round aircraft. By June 1944 both the 20th and 55th Fighter Groups had replaced all their P-38 Lightnings for

P-38F standing on the dispersal strip, Henderson Field, Guadalcanal.

the P-51 Mustang and by the end of the year all the other groups, with the exception of the 474th, had replaced their Lightnings. The 474th argued and pleaded successfully to retain their Lightnings and were the only Group so to do by the time the war in Europe ended in May 1945.

The end of the war in Europe may have ended, but the war with Japan was still raging although the Japanese Army was on the backfoot. The Allies were now pouring men and machines into the Pacific and had re-taken the Gilbert, Marshall and Marianas islands, and were in the process of encircling the Philippines. Pounded and strafed by bombers and fighter aircraft from the US 13th and 5th Air Forces, along with the Australians and New Zealanders, slowly but surely the ring closed in around the Japanese strongholds of Rabaul and Truk. Three times the desperate Japanese forces attempted to break-out and suffered horrendous losses. On the Islands of New Britain and the Carolines, the Japanese were rapidly running out of food and fuel as the Allies took control of the skies and the surrounding

P-38L (F-5G conversion) at Kanwang Airfield, Shangai, China.

seas, preventing supplies from getting to them.

There was also a `forgotten war' still being fought in Burma and China and two Lightning squadrons, the 449th and 459th, were in the thick of that. The two squadrons had been formed in North Africa in July 1943 and had volunteered to take their aircraft to China to join up with Brigadier-General Claire Chennault's 14th Air Force in Kunming. There they joined up with the 23rd Fighter Group who had replaced the worn-out legendary 'Flying Tigers' the previous July. The 459th Fighter Squadron later joined up with the 80th Fighter Group and was redesignated the 4th Squadron.

Enemy air opposition was sporadic to say the least and the vast majority of the missions carried out by the two squadrons was against enemy supply lines. Occasionally they were involved in dogfights and in one of these, one of the pilots, Lieutenant Tom Harmon a former football star, was shot down. Despite suffering from extensive burns he managed to walk back to his base, taking 32 days to do so. Quite a remarkable feat considering not only the hostile terrain, but its hostile inhabitants.

The 459th Fighter Squadron, or 'Twin Dragons', as it was known, was part of the 10th Air Force, which was under the command of General Lewis Brereton. Their primary function was to fly as escort to the Air Transport Command C-47s that flew over the Himalayas to China, in support of Chiang Kai-shek and the 14th Air Force. These 'Over the Hump' pilots, as they were known, had an onerous task inasmuch as if they ran into difficulties on their missions the terrain below them offered little or no support. The sight of the P-38 Lightnings flying as escort for them must

Captain Walter F Duke of the 459th FS 'Twin Dragons', scored 13 aerial victories.

have been one of the most re-assuring.

Supporting Allied operations in Northern Burma was one of the most difficult of operations because of the dense jungle. Two Allied guerilla groups, US General Frank Merrill's 'Merrill's Marauders' and British General Orde Wingate's 'Chindits', operated in the jungle harassing the retreating

P-38L-5 with the camera nose section of an F-5 at Shanghai,China.

F-5E of the US 10th Air Force at Hangchoa Airfield, China.

Japanese army. When opportunities arose, the P-38 Lightnings were called in to strafe Japanese supply lines and to protect Allied supply drops.

In March 1944 the 459th Fighter Squadron `Twin Dragons' was moved to India to join up with the RAF's 224 Group at Chittagong on the Bay of Bengal. In the following two months the squadron destroyed 126 Japanese aircraft, but during the following 10 months, only produced 30 victories. This highlighted the fact that Japan was running out of aircraft and pilots and they were in dire trouble.

The P-38 Lightning squadrons and groups were going through changes. As their aircraft were lost they were not being replaced, so the 9th Fighter Squadron of the 49th Fighter Group and the 39th Fighter Squadron of the 35th Fighter Group had all their aircraft replaced with P-47 Thunderbolts. All their aircraft in turn were given to the 475th Fighter Group to re-equip their three fighter squadrons the 431st, 432nd and 433rd and bring them up to strength. Together with the 35th, 36th and 80th Fighter Squadron of the 8th Fighter Group, these were the only two groups in the US 5th Air Force equipped with P-38 Lightnings.

Such was the outcry from the pilots of the squadrons, that in May 1944 the 9th Fighter Squadron was re-equipped with P-38J-15 Lightnings. The remaining squadrons in the 49th Fighter Group were re-equipped with P-38J-25s in September 1944. Although in Europe the Lightning squadrons were being phased out, in the Pacific Theatre some of the P-40 groups were being re-equipped with the new P-38s. One of these was the 18th Fighter Group from the 13th Air Force which was assigned, along with the 347th

F-5G at Shangai.

Fighter Group, to the force that was about to carry out an assault on the Philippines.

Among the 475th Fighter Group were three outstanding pilots, all of which were destined to become `top aces', but were as different as chalk and cheese – Lieutenant-Colonel Thomas J Lynch, Major Thomas McGuire and Major Richard Bong. Lynch was a professional soldier, a disciplinarian and a born leader and was respected by everyone who came into contact with him. Bong on the other hand was a happy-go-lucky type full of enthusiasm. Liked by everyone including General Kenney who allowed Bong a certain amount of freedom whilst in the air, which was tantamount to allowing him *carte blanche*. The third one, another P-38 pilot, Major Thomas B McGuire, who had seen action in the Aleutian islands, was running a close third. McGuire was one of those men whose ability and skill as a fighter pilot was beyond question, but his intolerant attitude toward his fellow pilots was one that was to make him disliked. Nothing short of perfection was acceptable and nobody satisfied him or came up to the standards he demanded. McGuire was killed on 7 January 1945, when his aircraft stalled at low altitude whilst chasing a Japanese Zero, he was awarded a posthumous Congressional Medal of Honor.

On 8 March 1944 Lieutenant-Colonel Lynch was killed by the returning fire from the ship he was attacking. He had 21 victories at the time. Throughout the summer months the squadrons carried out strafing raids on enemy positions, but rarely came into contact with Japanese aircraft. Lightnings from the 6th Photo-reconnaissance Squadron began a series of

F-5E in Italy about to land after a reconnaissance flight.

F-5 of the 5th Photographic Reconnaissance Group, 23rd Photo-reconnaissance Squadron.

A P-38 Lightning of the 475th FG, over the Markam Valley, New Guinea.

missions to map the Leyte area in the central Philippines in preparation for the invasion of the islands. This was followed some days later by a strike on the Japanese oil installations in Balikpapan, Borneo. In a desperate attempt to prevent the destruction of their vital oil facilities, the Japanese mustered as many fighters as they could manage to attack the Allied bombers of the Far East Air Force. The 49th Fighter Group, who were attached to the 5th Air Force at the time, accompanied 58 Consolidated B-24 Liberators on the raid and shot down two Japanese aircraft, a twin-engined Kawasaki Ki-45 Type 2 and a Nakajima Ki-43 Type 1. A second raid four days later resulted in four more Japanese aircraft with no losses to the Allies.

Then on 20 October 1944 the invasion of the Philippines began as General

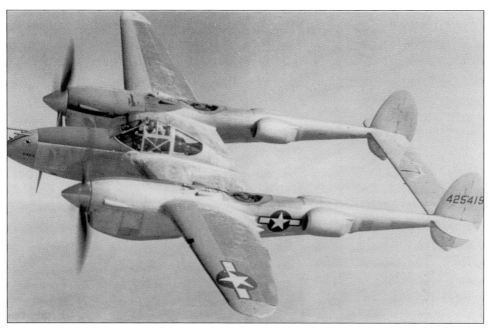

The P-38L-5-LO in its natural aluminium finish, on a test flight over California.

Douglas MacArthur's American and Australian troops went ashore at Tacloban and Dulag on the Leyte Gulf. Within days of the landings an airstrip had been prepared with a 2,800 feet steel mat runway and, as the last mat was laid into position, 34 P-38J Lightnings of the 49th Fighter Group landed.

The appearance of a new model of the P-38 Lightning, the P-38L, had all the pilots waiting in anticipation. According to the manufacturers it had a 2,000 feet higher ceiling than the existing P-38Js, it was faster, had tail-mounted radar to warn the pilot of any unwelcome surprises from the rear and more powerful engines. The tail mounted radar system, AN/APS-13, was fitted in the aft section of the left tail boom. When an aircraft approached from behind the transmitter-receiver system it was picked up by the radar in a cone mounted behind the P-38L. A warning bell sounded in the cockpit and a red warning light flashed alongside the gunsight enabling the pilot to take evasive action. Well that was the theory. What they didn't say was that the aircraft was also 500-lb heavier, so the overall performance improvements were not a great deal better that the P-38 Lightnings already in service. With the addition of two 300 gallon drop tanks however, the range of the L model was 2,600 miles above 10,000 feet, which was an improvement on the earlier models. This was one of the biggest single production orders of 3,924 P-38L-LO (the LO referred to Lockheed) this included 113 P-38L-5-VNs (VN refers to Vultee-Nashville, a division of Consolidated Vultee). There was a further order for 1,887 P-38Ls

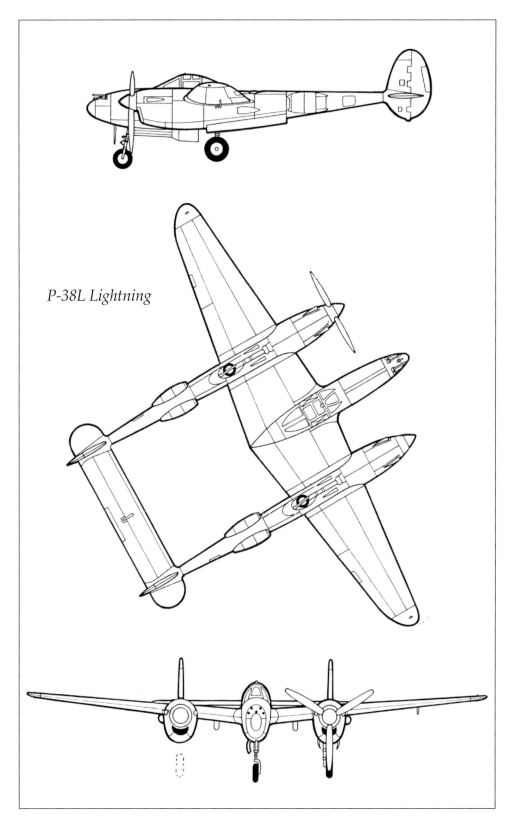

P-38L Lightning

The new improved P-38L-5

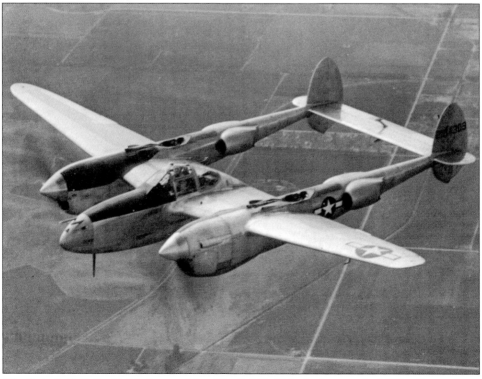

The fastest of all the Lightning models - The P-38J. It had a top speed of 420 miles per hour.

in the pipeline for Consolidated Vultee, but these were cancelled due to the end of the war.

Seventy-Five of the P-38Ls were converted into night fighters and re-designated P-38M. Painted a deep glossy black, the aircraft were modified to take a second crew member, a radar operator, who sat behind and in a slightly raised position to that of the pilot. A bulbous canopy gave the radar operator quite a reasonable amount of head-and-shoulder room. The radar scanner was mounted in a streamlined housing and hung beneath the nose

The P-38M Night Lightning with its radar housed in a pod beneath the nose as can be seen in this photograph.

in a bomb-release shackle, just ahead of the nose landing gear. In an effort to reduce the flashback from the nozzles of the guns, flash nozzles were fitted, but with limited success. Experiments were also carried out to shield the flaming exhausts of the turbo-superchargers but were unsuccessful. Very little is known of the success or failure of the P-38M, but it is known that they saw combat against the Japanese in the Pacific.

Throughout November 1944 the P-38 Lightning Groups, with the exception of the 347th, were in constant use attacking shipping convoys that were attempting to supply the besieged Japanese Army with ammunition and supplies. They also carried out strafing runs in support of the Allied armies that were moving slowly but surely through the Philippines. The 347th Fighter Group carried out raids on the shipbuilding facilities in the Makassar district of the Celebes and also carried out attacks on the oil refineries at Tarakan, Borneo.

On 7 December 1944, three years to the day when Pearl Harbor was attacked, the battle by the Allies to secure Leyte began. The date had been chose deliberately by the Americans as their moment of reprisal for that infamous day. The amphibious assault was supported by virtually every available fighter aircraft in the area, P-38 Lightnings, P-47 Thunderbolts,

The P-38M was a modification of the P-38L-5-LO, equipped with radar and two seats, and came into service during the last weeks of the Pacific war.

P-40 Warhawks and Navy F4U Corsairs, who were tasked to take care of either enemy aircraft or to strafe and bomb the Japanese positions in support of the landings. The task of taking care of the Japanese air opposition fell to P-38 Lightnings of the 49th and 475th Fighter Groups. Such was the success of the landings, that Admiral Kincaid, USN, was given to remark 'that it was the finest air support he had ever seen in the south-west Pacific'.

The fighting was some of the most vicious of the war with no quarter given either in the air or on the ground. During one incident however, Lieutenant-Colonel Gerald Johnson of the 49th Fighter Group and his squadron, came upon a large number of Japanese fighters about to attack Allied positions. Together with his wingman, Lieutenant James Watkins and the other members of his squadron, they attacked the enemy fighters. The Japanese fighters were taken by surprise and were decimated destroying a large number of the enemy force. What was left of the Japanese fighters quickly left the area, with the exception of one Japanese pilot who continued to fight against overwhelming odds. With their fuel low and their ammunition exhausted, the American fighters gave up and moved away. Lieutenant-Colonel Johnson looked at the shot-up, battered Japanese Zero that was circling below him and swooped down. As he flew alongside he glanced at the Japanese pilot and waggled the wings of his aircraft in acknowledgement of a respected opponent, the Japanese pilot responded in a like manner and both went their respective ways.

P-38 fighter ace Major Dick Bong inspecting the dive recovery flaps that enabled the P-38J and L models to dive more safely and at steeper angles.

F-5 `Stinky' of the 9th Photographic Reconnaissance Squadron, 7th Bomber Group at Pandaveswar, India in 1943.

Armourer re-arming a P-38 Lightning. Note the muzzle covers already placed over the ends of the barrels.

As the war progressed and the Allied continued their relentless push against the rapidly declining Japanese forces, Major Richard Bong shot down his 40th confirmed Japanese aircraft. General Kenney, anxious for the families in the United States to have a hero, ordered Bong back to the United States so that he could be honoured by his countrymen. It was to be a short lived experience as Bong was killed flying a Lockheed P-80 Shooting Star just six months later.

P-38M (Night-fighter) conversion still in original paint scheme.

The Allied commanders decided that it was time for an all-out assault on Japan and started by taking Iwo Jima in the Bonin Islands and Okinawa in the Ryukyus. In preparation for the attacks two F-5 Lightnings from the 28th Photo-reconnaissance Squadron, accompanied by twelve P-38L Lightnings, carried out a series of mapping flights to get the necessary information on the Japanese positions. Some of the passes were made at heights of just 50 feet above ground level, but, the information was vital, as risks had to be taken. On 19 January 1945, two US Marine divisions went ashore and took part in one of the bloodiest battles of the Pacific war. The battles for these two objectives have been the subject of numerous books and films, they were possibly the fiercest battles of the war in the Pacific and the cost in lives horrendous. With the two bases in Allied hands it was only a stepping stone to Japan. Long-range B-17 and B-25 bombers of the 20th Air Force were tasked with the bombing missions, but it was realised that the P-47 Thunderbolts from the 318th Fighter Group that had been assigned as escorts, did not have sufficient range to carry out their duties. The answer was to create another P-38 Lightning unit and 30 P-38L Lightnings were assigned to the group and spread amongst its three squadrons the 19th, 33rd and 73rd.

After a minimum of familiarization the pilots carried out their first escort mission when 26 B-24 Liberators attacked Truk. Intercepted by a mixture of Japanese fighters the P-38 Lightnings accounted for six without loss. The results were encouraging so all the Lightnings in the group were brought together and formed into the Lightning Provisional Group. Two days after

F-5A-1 of the 343rd Fighter Group in the Aleutian Islands.

the formation of the group, they accompanied B-24 Liberators on a raid of the Japanese position on Iwo Jima. With no contact with Japanese fighter, the P-38 Lightnings decided to carry out strafing sorties during which one of the Lightnings, flown by Lieutenant Fred Erbele, took a hit on his left engine and another hit left a large hole in his right wing. His cockpit canopy also took a hit and was shattered exposing him to the elements.

Because of the damage the aircraft's speed was reduced to 135 mph and it was soon realised that the other Lightnings could not escort him home. Then two of the B-24 Liberators that he had been escorting, dropped down on either side of him, lowered their flaps and indicated to him that they would escort him part the way home. All went reasonably well until they hit a tropical storm. With the aircraft vibrating wildly and the rain lashing in, Lieutenant Erbele considered ditching, but then the rain cleared and waiting for him were two P-47 Thunderbolts who took over from the

F-5 of the 28th Fighter Squadron, 7th Photographic Group on Ulithi Atoll.

Liberators and escorted him into Saipan. He had been flying his battered Lightning for 4 hours and 20 minutes and had just 20 minutes fuel left on landing. This was not a one-off incident, but similar to many that had occurred throughout the war, but what this highlighted was the robustness of the P-38 Lightning and the determination of the men who flew it.

On the 1 April 1945 US Marines invaded the island of Okinawa, but it became a harder nut to crack than any they had encountered before. The island was a maze of tunnels and caves and took until 21 June before it was finally secured. The war was essentially over as the Japanese could retreat no further and in the final months of the war the P-38 Lightning squadrons hunted for stragglers but found very few. With the dropping of atomic

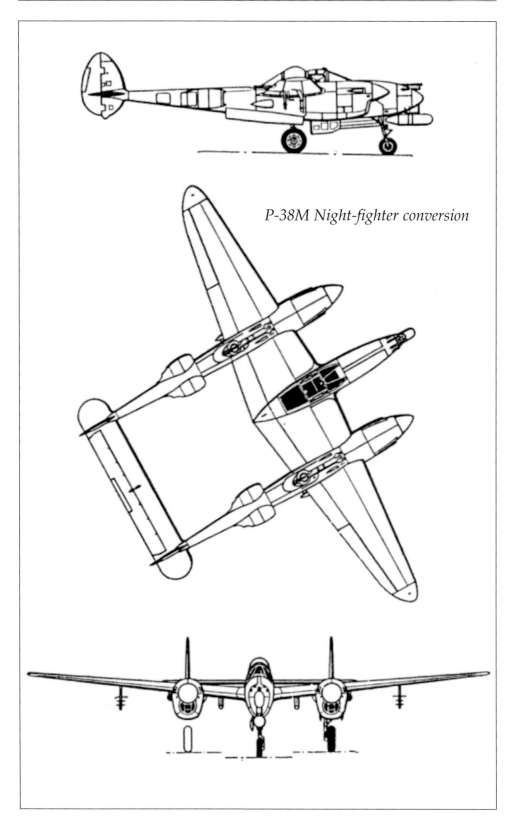

P-38M Night-fighter conversion

bombs on Hiroshima and Nagasaki the Japanese capitulated. It has been argued that it was an unnecessary act as the Japanese were beaten and starving, but the fanaticism of the Japanese soldier would have meant that they would not have accepted surrender easily and it was deemed that the dropping of the bombs shortened the war and saved many Allied lives.

It was felt fitting that the first USAAF fighter aircraft to land on Japanese soil after V-J Day should be the P-38 Lightning, after all it had been a major factor in the destruction of the Japanese Army Air Force.

The Lockheed P-38 Lightning saw action on every major battlefront and was one of the most feared fighter aircraft in the Pacific and Mediterranean Theatres of the Second World War. It became the springboard for a new generation of fighters that followed in its wake.

APPENDIX A

P-38 Lightning Variants

XP-38   The prototype model of the P-38 Lightning.

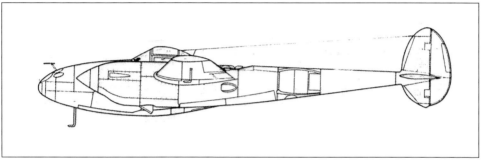

XP-38

YP-38   The replacement model for the XP-38 fitted with both machine-guns and cannon.

An underside view of the YP-38.

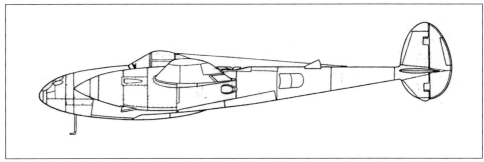

YP-38

P-38-LO   The first production model of the P-38 Lightning.

XP-38A   Production model fitted with a type of pressurised cockpit.

P-38D-LO   Production model featured with self-sealing fuel tanks with improved armour plating.

P-38E-LO   Production model with a 37-mm cannon instead of the 20-mm canon. Had improved electrical and hydraulic systems.

P-38E

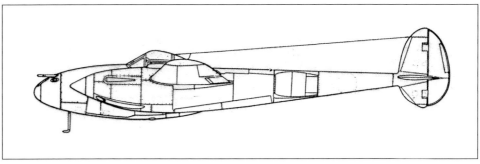

P-322-61

P-322-61   The RAF Lightning I was basically a P-38E without the turbo-superchargers. The finished aircraft was not delivered to the RAF as most ended as trainers and experimental models.

P-38F-LO   The first production models to be deemed to be combat ready straight from the production line.

P-38F-1-LO   As the previous model but fitted with under wing mounts capable of carrying two 165 gallon auxiliary fuel tanks or two 1,000 pound bombs. The underwing mounts were in the form of kits that were sent to the squadrons.

P-38F

F-4-1-LO   This was a modified P-38E powered by two V-1710-21/-29 engines and fitted with four K-17 cameras in the nose in place of the machine-guns and cannons. 99 of this version was used in the main for training.

F-4A-1-LO   This was an improved version of the above and was fitted with two 1,325 hp V-1710-49/-53 engines and fitted with four trimetrogon K-17 cameras which had the capability of photographing downwards and sideways. 20 of this version were built.

P-38F-5-LO   As the previous model but with factory fitted underwing mounts.

P-38F-13P   38 production models ordered by the Royal Air Force, but not
&15-LO   fitted with the turbo-superchargers. It was the lack of the turbo-superchargers that caused the RAF to reject the aircraft although their name for the aircraft, Lightning, was adopted by the Americans.

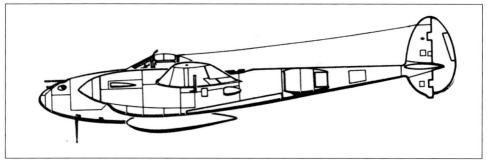

P-38F

F-5A-2-LO	Only one of this version was built and was developed as the prototype for the F-5A series and was powered by two 1,150 hp V-1710-21/-29 engines.
F-5A-1-LO	Twenty of this version were built and were powered by two 1,325 hp V-1710-51/-55 engines. They were also equipped with five cameras, four K-17s and one K-24.
F-5A-3-LO	As above. 20 produced.

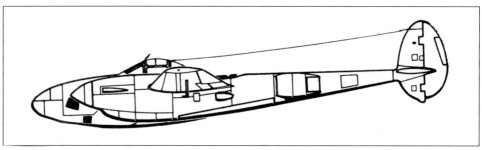

P-5A-10-LO

F-5A-10 shows under-nose detail of camera ports.

F-5A-10-LO   As above. 20 produced.

F-5B-1-LO   Almost identical to the above with the exception of two more powerful engines V-1710-89/-91s. 200 of these aircraft were built.

F-5C   Almost identical to the F-5A just with some minor modifications to the instrumentation.

XF-5D   A two-seat, armed photo-reconnaissance fighter.

Prototype XF-5D 'Bobbie'. Camera bulge under the nose.

F-5E-1-LO   100 of these modified P-38J-15-LOs were built and equipped with K-18 and 18 cameras.

F-5E-3-LO   105 of these aircraft were built and were modified P-38J-25-LOs. Like the F-5E-i-LO they were fitted with K-17 and 18 cameras.

F-5E conversion of a P-38J

F-5E-4-LO   500 of these aircraft were built and were modified from the P-38L-1-LO. and like the previous two models were fitted with the K-17 and 18 cameras. All three versions were unarmed.

F-5F   Built from the F-5B-1-LO only one prototype was manufactured and featured a completely different camera layout.

F-5G-6-LO   63 models of this aircraft were built all of which were modified P-38L-5-LOs. These had a different camera arrangement.

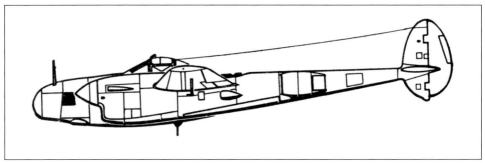

F-5G

FO-1   Four of these photo-reconnaissance Lightnings were built under strict secrecy and no details are available. All that is known is that they were destined for the North African Theatre of the war and had been procured by the US Navy.

P-38G-1-LO   This was the same version as the P-38F-15-LO but with a much improved radio and oxygen system. Only 80 built.

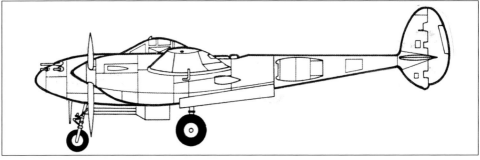

P-38G

P-38G-3-LO   As the above version but fitted with a new model turbo-supercharger. Only 12 built.

P-38G-5-LO.   As above but with improved instrumentation only 68 built.

P-38G-10-LO. Production model fitted with underwing racks capable of carrying twelve 4.5-inch rockets in four three-tube launchers. The racks could be adapted to carry two 1,600 pound bombs or two 165 gallon drop tanks. Some of these models were fitted with special equipment for operation in cold climates. 548 were built.

P-38G-13-LO   Improved version of the previous G-models, 174 built.

This P-38 is equipped with 'Christmas Tree' type launching clusters.

P-38G-15-LO   This model was ordered by the RAF but never delivered. Model 322-60 was given the RAF designation Lightning II. 200 were built.

P-38H of the AAF Tactical Centre, Orlando, Florida

P-38H-1-LO. Improved version with 1,425-hp V-1710-89/-91 engines. 226 of this model were built.

P-38H-5-LO   As above but with 1,240-hp engines with the GE B-33 turbo-superchargers.

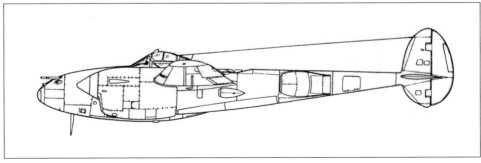

P-38J

P-38J-5-LO   This model had upgraded air cooler inlets giving the engine improved performance to the Allison V-1710-89/-91 engines. 210 versions of this model were built.

P-38J-10-LO.   As above only with the improved General Electric B-33 turbo-superchargers. The windscreen in front of the pilot was replaced with a bullet-proof flat screen. 790 were built.

P-38J

P-38J-15-LO   1,400 versions of this model were built and had a new electrical system and new turbo-supercharger governors.

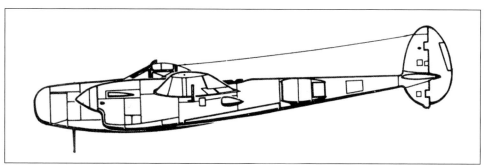

P-38J-15-LO (BTO)

P-38J-20-LO   Almost identical to the -15-LO, two of these were modified in Australia and fitted with AN/APS radar carried in a pod beneath the wing. A number were also modified to carry a

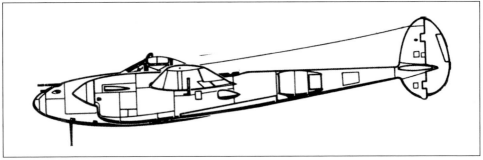

P-38J-20-LO

second crewman in an extended nose of the aircraft in place of the machine-guns and cannons. These models became known as `Droop Snoot' Lightnings. 350 of this model were manufactured.

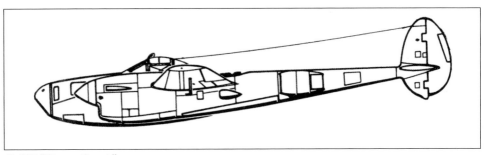

P-38J "Droop Snoot"

P-38J-25-LO   This model was the first one to be fitted with the electrically driven dive flaps and the hydraulically boosted and powered ailerons. 210 versions were built.

P-38K-LO   Only one of these models was built and that was a modified P-38G-10-LO fitted two 1,425-hp V-1710-75/-77 engines which turned two wide chord three-bladed propellers and had the General Electric B-14 turbo-superchargers.

P-38L-1-LO   These were almost identical to the production J models with the exception of the engines which were the Allison 1,425-hp V-1710-75/-77s.

P-38L-5-LO   These were `Droop Snoot' versions with the new engines and underwing racks capable of carrying two 2,000 pound bombs, ten 5-inch rockets or fuel drop tanks. 2,520 of these aircraft were ordered but the vast majority were never completed because of the end of the war.

P-38L 'Droop Snoop' with a bomb load six 5,000-lb missiles, August 1944

P-38L-5-VN   This was the only model of the P-38 Lightning that was not built by Lockheed. Only 113 of a 2,000 order of this version were built by the Consolidated-Vultee Aircraft Corporation in Nashville, Tennessee.

P-38M   The two-seater version of the P-38 and known as the 'Night Lightning'. Painted all-over glossy black and equipped with rocket, machine-guns and cannons, the P-38M also had AN/APS-6 radar. It was 37 mph faster than the Northrop Black Widow night fighter but arrived very late in the war and saw very little action.

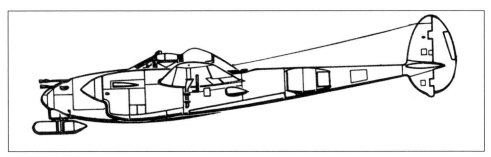

P-38M-5-LO

P-38M two-seat night-fighter with raised second cockpit.

XP-49   An early production P-38 was modified to fit the role of an advanced interceptor pursuit fighter. It featured a pressurized cockpit but after tests at the Wright-Patterson AFB, Dayton, Ohio, it was scrapped.

The XP-49.

APPENDIX B

P-38 Lightning Specifications

XP-38

Engines:	Two 1,150-hp turbo-supercharged Allison V-1710-11/15.
Wingspan:	52 feet (15.84 m).
Wing Area:	327.5 sq. ft. (30.42 m²).
Length:	37ft. 10in. (11.53 m).
Height:	12ft. 10in. (3.91 m).
Weight Empty:	11,507lb. (5,220 kg).
Weight Gross:	13,964lb. (6,334 kg).
Maximum Take-off Weight:	15,416lb. (6,993 kg).
Maximum Speedat 20,000ft:	413 mph (665 km/h).
Cruising Speed:	330 mph (531 km/h).
Landing Speed:	80 mph (129 km/h).
Climb Rate to 20,000ft:	6.5 minutes.
Service Ceiling:	38,000ft. (11,582 m).
Range:	890 miles (1,432 km).
Maximum Range:	1,390 miles (2,237 km).
Fuel (Normal):	210 US gallons (795 litres).
Fuel (Maximum):	400 US gallons (1,514 litres).
Armament:	Nil.

YP-38

Engines:	Two 1,150-hp turbo-supercharged Allison V-1710-27/29.
Wing span:	52 feet (15.84 m).
Wing Area:	327.5 sq. ft. (30.42 m²).
Length:	37ft. 10in. (11.53 m).

Height:	9ft. 10in. (2.98 m).
Weight Empty:	11,171lb. (5,067 kg).
Weight Gross:	13,500lb. (6,124 kg).
Maximum Take-off Weight:	14,348lb. (6,508 kg).
Maximum Speed at 20,000ft:	405 mph (652 km/h).
Cruising Speed:	330 mph (531 km/h).
Landing Speed:	80 mph (129 km/h).
Climb Rate to 20,000ft:	6 minutes.
Service Ceiling:	38,000ft. (11,582 m).
Range:	650 miles (1,046 km).
Maximum Range:	1,390 miles (2,237 km).
Fuel (Normal):	210 US gallons (795 litres).
Fuel (Maximum):	400 US gallons (1,514 litres).
Armament:	One 37-mm Cannon, two .50 calibre and two .30 calibre machine guns.

P-38

Engines:	Two 1,150-hp turbo-supercharged Allison V-1710-27/29.
Wing span:	52 feet (15.84 m).
Wing Area:	327.5 sq. ft. (30.42 m²).
Length:	37ft. 10in. (11.53 m).
Height:	12ft. 10in. (3.91 m).
Weight Empty:	11,672lb. (5,294 kg).
Weight Gross:	14,178lb. (6,431 kg).
Maximum Take-off Weight:	15,340lb. (6,958 kg).
Maximum Speed at 20,000ft:	395 mph (636 km/h).
Cruising Speed:	310 mph (499 km/h).
Landing Speed:	80 mph (129 km/h).
Climb Rate to 20,000ft:	6 minutes.
Service Ceiling:	25,000ft. (7,620 m).
Range:	825 miles (1,328 km).
Maximum Range:	1,490 miles (2,398 km).
Fuel (Normal):	210 US gallons (795 litres).

Fuel (Maximum): 400 US gallons (1,514 litres).

Armament: One 37-mm Cannon, four .50 calibre machine guns.

P-38D

Engines: Two 1,150-hp turbo-supercharged Allison V-1710-27/29.

Wing span: 52 feet (15.84 m).

Wing Area: 327.5 sq. ft. (30.42 m²).

Length: 37ft. 10in. (11.53 m).

Height: 12ft. 10in. (3.91 m).

Weight Empty: 11,780lb. (5,343 kg).

Weight Gross: 14,456lb. (6,557 kg).

Maximum Take-off Weight: 15,500lb. (7,031 kg).

Maximum Speed at 20,000ft: 390 mph (628 km/h).

Cruising Speed: 300 mph (483 km/h).

Landing Speed: 85 mph (137 km/h)

Climb Rate to 20,000ft: 8 minutes.

Service Ceiling: 39,000ft. (11,887 m).

Range: 500 miles (805 km).

Maximum Range: 975 miles (1,569 km).

Fuel (Normal): 210 US gallons (795 litres).

Fuel (Maximum): 300 US gallons (1,361 litres).

Armament: One 37-mm Cannon, four .50 calibre machine guns.

P-38E

Engines: Two 1,150-hp turbo-supercharged Allison V-1710-27/29.

Wing span: 52 feet (15.84 m).

Wing Area: 327.5 sq. ft. (30.42 m²).

Length: 37ft. 10in. (11.53 m).

Height: 12ft. 10in. (3.91 m).

Weight Empty: 11,880lb. (5,389 kg).

Weight Gross:	14,424lb. (6,543 kg).
Maximum Take-off Weight:	15,482lb. (7,023 kg).
Maximum Speed at 20,000ft:	395 mph (636 km/h).
Cruising Speed:	300 mph (483 km/h).
Landing Speed:	85 mph (137 km/h)
Climb Rate to 20,000ft:	8 minutes.
Service Ceiling:	39,000ft. (11,887 m).
Range:	500 miles (805 km).
Maximum Range:	975 miles (1,569 km).
Fuel (Normal):	210 US gallons (795 litres).
Fuel (Maximum):	300 US gallons (1,361 litres).
Armament:	One 20-mm Cannon, four .50 calibre machine guns.

P-38 Lightning Mark I.

Engines:	Two 1,090-hp turbo-supercharged Allison V-1710-C15.
Wing span:	52 feet (15.84 m).
Wing Area:	327.5 sq. ft. (30.42 m²).
Length:	37ft. 10in. (11.53 m).
Height:	9ft. 10in. (2.99 m).
Weight Empty:	11,945lb. (5,418 kg).
Weight Gross:	14,467lb. (6,562 kg).
Maximum Take-off Weight:	15,482lb. (7,023 kg).
Maximum Speed at 20,000ft:	357 mph (575 km/h).
Cruising Speed:	300 mph (483 km/h).
Landing Speed:	85 mph (137 km/h)
Climb Rate to 20,000ft:	8 minutes.
Service Ceiling:	40,000ft. (12,192 m).
Range:	500 miles (805 km).
Maximum Range:	975 miles (1,569 km).
Fuel (Normal):	210 US gallons (795 litres).
Fuel (Maximum):	300 US gallons (1,361 litres).
Armament:	One 20-mm Cannon, four .50 calibre machine guns.

Close-up of redome installation on the P-38M Night Fighter.

P-38F

Engines:	Two 1,325-hp turbo-supercharged Allison V-1710-49/53
Wing span:	52 feet (15.84 m).
Wing Area:	327.5 sq. ft. (30.42 m²).
Length:	37ft. 10in. (11.53 m).
Height:	12ft. 10in. (3.91 m).
Weight Empty:	12,264lb. (5,563 kg).
Weight Gross:	15,900lb. (7,212 kg).
Maximum Take-off Weight:	18,000lb. (8,165 kg).
Maximum Speed at 20,000ft:	395 mph (636 km/h).
Cruising Speed:	305 mph (491 km/h).
Landing Speed:	85 mph (137 km/h)
Climb Rate to 20,000ft:	8 minutes.
Service Ceiling:	39,000ft. (11,887 m).
Range:	425 miles (684 km).
Maximum Range:	1,925 miles (3,098 km).
Fuel (Normal):	230 US gallons (871 litres).
Fuel (Maximum):	600 US gallons (2,271 litres).
Armament:	One 20-mm Cannon, four .50 calibre machine guns. 2,000lb. bombs.

P-38G

Engines:	Two 1,325-hp turbo-supercharged Allison V-1710-51/55
Wing span:	52 feet (15.84 m).
Wing Area:	327.5 sq. ft. (30.42 m²).
Length:	37ft. 10in. (11.53 m).
Height:	9ft. 10in. (2.99 m).
Weight Empty:	12,200lb. (5,534 kg).
Weight Gross:	15,800lb. (7,167 kg).
Maximum Take-off Weight:	19,800lb. (8,981 kg).
Maximum Speed at 20,000ft:	400 mph (644 km/h).

Cruising Speed:	340 mph (547 km/h).
Landing Speed:	85 mph (137 km/h)
Climb Rate to 20,000ft:	8.5 minutes.
Service Ceiling:	39,000ft. (11,887 m).
Range:	275 miles (443 km).
Maximum Range:	2,400 miles (3,862 km).
Fuel (Normal):	230 US gallons (871 litres).
Fuel (Maximum):	900 US gallons (3,406 litres).
Armament:	One 20-in.machine-gun, four .50 calibre machine guns. 3,200lb. bombs.

P-38H

Engines:	Two 1,325-hp turbo-supercharged Allison V-1710-89/91.
Wing span:	52 feet (15.84 m).
Wing Area:	327.5 sq. ft. (30.42 m²).
Length:	37ft. 10in. (11.53 m).
Height:	9ft. 10in. (2.99 m).
Weight Empty:	12,380lb. (5,616 kg).
Weight Gross:	16,300lb. (7,394 kg).
Maximum Take-off Weight:	20,300lb. (9,208 kg).
Maximum Speed at 20,000ft:	402 mph (647 km/h).
Cruising Speed:	250 mph (402 km/h).
Landing Speed:	88 mph (142 km/h)
Climb Rate to 20,000ft:	6.5 minutes.
Service Ceiling:	40,000ft. (12,192 m).
Range:	350 miles (563 km).
Maximum Range:	2,400 miles (3,862 km).
Fuel (Normal):	230 US gallons (871 litres).
Fuel (Maximum):	900 US gallons (3,406 litres).
Armament:	One 20-mm cannon, four .50 calibre machine guns. 3,200lb.bombs.

P-38J

Engines:	Two 1,325-hp turbo-supercharged Allison V-1710-89/91.
Wing span:	52 feet (15.84 m).
Wing Area:	327.5 sq. ft. (30.42 m^2).
Length:	37ft. 10in. (11.53 m).
Height:	9ft. 10in. (2.99 m).
Weight Empty:	12,780lb. (5,797 kg).
Weight Gross:	17,500lb. (7,938 kg).
Maximum Take-off Weight:	21,600lb. (9,798 kg).
Maximum Speed at 20,000ft:	414 mph (666 km/h).
Cruising Speed:	290 mph (467 km/h).
Landing Speed:	105 mph (169 km/h)
Climb Rate to 20,000ft:	7 minutes.
Service Ceiling:	44,000ft. (13,411 m).
Range:	450 miles (724 km).
Maximum Range:	2,600 miles (4,184 km).

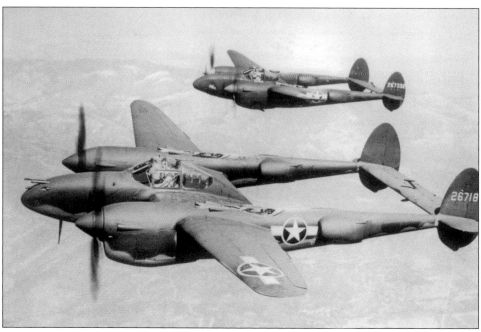

A P-38J-5-LO bristling with cannon and machine guns together with the unarmed photo-reconnaissance version the F-5B-1-LO.

Fuel (Normal):	410 US gallons (1,552 litres).
Fuel (Maximum):	1,010 US gallons (3,823 litres).
Armament:	One 20-mm cannon, four .50 calibre machine guns. 3,200lb. bombs.

P-38L

Engines:	Two 1,325-hp turbo-supercharged Allison V-1710-111/113.
Wing span:	52 feet (15.84 m).
Wing Area:	327.5 sq. ft. (30.42 m^2).
Length:	37ft. 10in. (11.53 m).
Height:	9ft. 10in. (2.99 m).
Weight Empty:	12,800lb. (5,806 kg).
Weight Gross:	17,500lb. (7,938 kg).
Maximum Take-off Weight:	21,600lb. (9,798 kg).
Maximum Speed at 20,000ft:	414 mph (666 km/h).
Cruising Speed:	290 mph (467 km/h).
Landing Speed:	105 mph (169 km/h)
Climb Rate to 20,000ft:	7 minutes.
Service Ceiling:	44,000ft. (13,411 m).
Range:	450 miles (724 km).
Maximum Range:	2,600 miles (4,184 km).
Fuel (Normal):	410 US gallons (1,552 litres).
Fuel (Maximum):	1,010 US gallons (3,823 litres).
Armament:	One 20-mm cannon, four .50 calibre machine guns . 3,200lb. bombs.

P-38M

Engines:	Two 1,325-hp turbo-supercharged Allison V-1710-111/113.
Wing span:	52 feet (15.84 m).
Wing Area:	327.5 sq. ft. (30.42 m^2).
Length:	40ft. 1in. (12.03 m).
Height:	9ft. 10in. (2.99 m).
Weight Empty:	12,800lb. (5,806 kg).

Weight Gross:	18,830lb. (9,938 kg).
Maximum Take-off Weight:	21,600lb. (9,798 kg).
Maximum Speed at 20,000ft:	458 mph (696 km/h).
Cruising Speed:	290 mph (467 km/h).
Landing Speed:	105 mph (169 km/h)
Climb Rate to 20,000ft:	7 minutes.
Service Ceiling:	44,000ft. (13,411 m).
Range:	450 miles (724 km).
Maximum Range:	2,600 miles (4,184 km).
Fuel (Normal):	410 US gallons (1,552 litres).
Fuel (Maximum):	1,010 US gallons (3,823 litres).
Armament:	One 20-mm cannon, four .50 calibre machine guns 3,200lb. bombs.
Crew:	Two - Pilot and Radar Operator.